Airstream Memories

John Brunkowski & Michael Closen

Schiffer Publishing Ltd

4880 Lower Valley Road • Atglen, PA 19310

Other Schiffer Books By The Authors:
Pictorial Guide to RVing. ISBN: 9780764335464. $24.99

Other Schiffer Books on Related Subjects:
Airstreams: Custom Interiors. David Winick. ISBN: 9780764335396. $29.99

Copyright © 2012 by John Brunkowski & Michael Closen

Library of Congress Control Number: 2012943032

Designed by RoS
Type set in Chalet-NewYorkNineteenSeventy/Zurich BT

ISBN: 978-0-7643-4163-2
Printed in China

Schiffer Books are available at special discounts for bulk purchases for sales promotions or premiums. Special editions, including personalized covers, corporate imprints, and excerpts can be created in large quantities for special needs. For more information contact the publisher:

Published by Schiffer Publishing, Ltd.
4880 Lower Valley Road
Atglen, PA 19310
Phone: (610) 593-1777; Fax: (610) 593-2002
E-mail: Info@schifferbooks.com

For the largest selection of fine reference books on this and related subjects, please visit our website at **www.schifferbooks.com**
We are always looking for people to write books on new and related subjects. If you have an idea for a book, please contact us at proposals@schifferbooks.com

This book may be purchased from the publisher.
Please try your bookstore first.
You may write for a free catalog.

In Europe, Schiffer books are distributed by
Bushwood Books
6 Marksbury Ave.
Kew Gardens
Surrey TW9 4JF England
Phone: 44 (0) 20 8392 8585; Fax: 44 (0) 20 8392 9876
E-mail: info@bushwoodbooks.co.uk
Website: www.bushwoodbooks.co.uk

CONTENTS

FOREWORD– 4

INTRODUCTION– 6

Chapter 1– **Airstream Background** –9

Chapter 2– **Airstream Advertising** –23

Chapter 3– **Airstream At Rest** –37

Chapter 4– **Airstream Aerials** –47

Chapter 5– **Airstream Pieces** –57

Chapter 6– **Airstream On The Road & Roadside** –67

Chapter 7– **Airstream Parks & Rallies** –77

Chapter 8– **Airstream International** –89

Chapter 9– **Airstream Look-A-Likes** –99

Chapter 10– **Airstream Art & Humor** –111

BIBLIOGRAPHY– 128

FOREWORD

Rich Luhr, Editor, *AIRSTREAM LIFE*

With this, their latest book, authors John Brunkowski and Michael Closen have taken on a most monumental task: answering the question, "Why are Airstreams icons?"

As Editor of *AIRSTREAM LIFE* magazine, I've struggled with that question for years. The possible answers seem obvious at first—decades of Airstream history, famous globetrotting caravans, the travel choice of star and statesman, enduring modernist design, long-lasting aluminum shells—and, most probably, all of those things together. But, when you try to verbalize exactly how all that turns into the status of "icon," suddenly the words ring hollow and the explanation becomes elusive. It seems that only those who love Airstreams can fully understand the connection we feel to these inanimate objects.

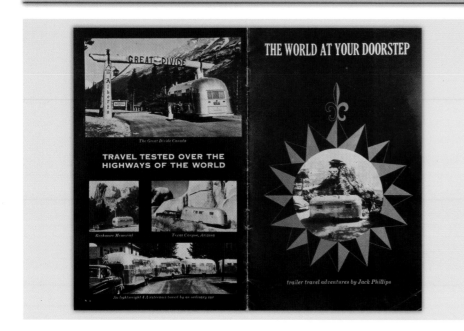

Advertising Brochure [front on the right & back on the left]. Standard brochure paper, real black & white photos [21 of them], bi-fold design, 10.5" x 8.25" unfolded [5.25' x 8.25' folded], by Jack Phillips & Airstream, 16 pages, unnumbered, c. 1950s. Titled: "The World At Your Doorstep." This rare, vintage sales pamphlet legitimately claimed that Airstream had been "travel tested over the highways of the world." Like this outstanding old paper item, our book is filled with vintage and newer pieces of advertising and memorabilia, produced by Airstream and other sources. And, much like the caption you are reading, each piece will be described in some detail—ending in every instance with an estimated valuation such as follows. $25-50.

Collector Plate. Porcelain dinner plate, 10.75" round, shades of gray graphics, by artist Antar Bayal & 222 Fifth, "Slice of Life" pattern, entitled "Lunar Barbecue," #2638871, c. 1990s-2000s. This creative tribute to Airstream on a piece of historically and futuristically themed dinnerware stands as a representative example of the types of Airstream items and images included throughout this book. The plate shows a person in a space suit standing at a barbeque, on the Moon, with the Earth in the background, and standing next to a handsome tandem-axle Airstream Land Yacht. The text on the back of this plate is extraordinarily thoughtful and perceptive. It reads, in part: "Poking a bit of fun at all of the illustrations through time that attempted to depict the future 'achievements' of human kind. The artist draws upon the classic logic of projecting the known into the unknown. After all, if you were thinking from a perspective of 1950, what would make better sense than an Airstream trailer as the first moon base." $20-25.

Much like a polished Airstream's reflective shell, which shines brilliantly and yet paradoxically blends into the background by reflecting its own surroundings, the Airstream is iconic primarily because it reflects Americana at so many levels. I think the love of Airstream is a result of how it enables us to fulfill our own desires to escape the humdrum, to have adventures, and to re-connect with our family and friends—and with ourselves.

But you can decide for yourself. In this book, Brunkowski and Closen attempt to answer the question of why Airstreams are icons, through a study of collectibles and memorabilia. Yes, Airstreams long ago reached the level of cultural esteem where they have spun off thousands of pieces of memorabilia. It may be that the best way to understand the mystique is to look at what surrounds the Airstream, instead of looking at only the Airstream itself.

Brunkowski and Closen seem to think so. By documenting our tokens, photos, totems, and art, they tell a story about how America has perceived the Airstream, and more importantly, what the Airstream has revealed about us through the decades. Read on, and discover both Airstream history and how our classically American love of Airstream tells a story about ourselves.

Advertising Brochure. Standard brochure construction, real multi-color photos & graphics, 8.25" x 11", by Airstream, 38 pages, unnumbered, copyright 1976. Titled: *The Airstream Story*. For years, Airstream published annually a comparable, classy, and substantial brochure that included both information about Airstream philosophy and history and information about its then-current fleet of trailers. These annual works have become valuable historical background pieces and highly popular collectibles. Each annual brochure included numerous quality color photographs—mostly taken through the mid-1970s by Airstream's exceptional photographer Ardean Miller. A number of these brochures will be displayed in this book, and the picture on the cover of this particular brochure appears on a postcard shown later in our book. $50-75.

Advertising Postcard. Unused, real color photo & multi-color graphics, 6" x 4.25", by Samsung, unnumbered, copyright 2005. This bright and revealing card publicized both Samsung telephones and the downtown Miami, Florida, nightclub Club Pawn Shop Miami. Notice the Samsung cell phone held by the attractive dancer. The fun theme of this club that opened in 2004 was nostalgia—which filled the inside of the former pawnshop occupied by the nightclub. Included in the building's vast array of vintage items was a 1960s Airstream trailer, as pictured in the background on this scarce postcard. Over the last eight decades, it has been a great tribute to Airstream that so many other businesses and organizations have chosen to include Airstream trailer images in their publicity pieces, such as this card. We have included about 285 postcards in this book, some 95% of which picture Airstreams and most of which were produced for entities other than Airstream. $20-25.

INTRODUCTION

Several excellent books have been published about Airstream travel trailers, and they are listed in our Bibliography. But, this book is the first to tell the Airstream story through hundreds of postcards and other pieces of memorabilia. Over some twenty-five years of RVing, we have collected thousands of RV-related items, including several hundred Airstream items, and every piece shown in this book is part of our RV collection. We are proud to have authored two other books and several articles about RVing, and we have written briefly about Airstream in some of those publications. One of the three RVs we currently own is a vintage 1966 Airstream Safari, and we love all things Airstream. So, we hope to provide you with some images, some information, and some thoughts about Airstream that you have not seen, or read, or considered before. This book is about both Airstream itself and the mystique

Advertising Brochure [underneath]. Construction paper, tri-fold design (6 sides), multi-color graphics, small 3" x 6" folded [9" x 6" unfolded], by Wally Byam's Trailer Supplies, unnumbered, c. 1960. Caption: "Announcing the most authoritative book on Trailer Travel." This rare little paper item served as one of the promotional pieces for Wally Byam's historic 1960 book *Trailer Travel Here And Abroad,* which is displayed in one of the next pictures and which describes many of his famous international caravans. Byam was a master as an author and a genius as a promoter—either of which skills would fit appropriately on the commemorative coin shown here as well. $20-25.

Collector Coin [on top]. Shiny lightweight silver metal, two-sided circular design, raised graphics, 1.5" diameter, by Airstream, unnumbered, dated 1976. Front caption: "Airstream Founder and World Traveler Wally Byam." This handsome non-monetary coin showed the bust of Wally Byam and was produced for the celebration of the USA Bicentennial in 1976. Although no maker is actually disclosed on the coin, we presume it was Airstream because of the language appearing on the reverse side of the coin, as follows: "Go Airstream for a better life, more independence and the greater pursuit of happiness." $15-20.

Bolo Tie Medallion. Heavy metal, multi-color graphics, 1.5" diameter, by WBCCI, unnumbered, c. 1980s-90s. Inscription: "WBCCI Unit Past President." This impressive crest served as the clasp to hold the two ends of a bolo tie together. Wally Byam Caravan Club International produced these bolo tie medallions, with the image of Wally Byam wearing the famous Blue Beret, to honor those individuals who had served as presidents of their local WBCCI groups. On the very first international caravan led by Wally Byam, which traveled to Mexico in the 1950s, he distributed blue berets to all of the participants in order to help identify them in crowds of people. $15-20.

surrounding it. We especially hope our book is not only informative, but also entertaining.

We only wish we had become of age in time to have met, and perhaps even gotten to know, Wally Byam. He somehow managed in his vast creation of Airstream to have bottled up travel adventure and to have marketed it effectively to the world. He was very bright, highly educated, and quite worldly. He grew up in the era of the real beginning of development of the recreational vehicle, and he was savvy enough to truly understand the big picture about matters affecting RVs. Those of us who now look back to the early decades of the 1900s cannot really appreciate the complex circumstances. Times were changing rapidly, and things were not as primitive as we might think. By the 1920s, RVing was here to stay—in the forms of auto camping, homemade travel trailers [and a few homemade "motorhomes"], and some commercially made coaches.

Already by the 1920s, magazines and books about auto camping and RVing were being published; tens of thousands of RVs had been constructed; thousands of campgrounds had been established. In 1925, for example, the authors of the book *Camping By The Highway: Autocampers' Handbook And Directory Of Camp Sites* wrote: "During

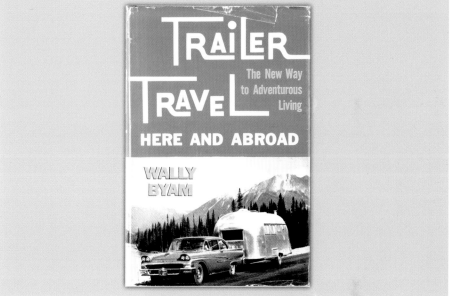

Vintage RV Book. Cloth cover and standard paper, black & white graphics, small 5" x 7", by George Sutton, Myron Briggs & Field & Stream Publishing, 160 pages, copyright 1925. Title: *Camping By The Highway: Autocampers' Handbook And Directory Of Camp Sites*. This rare book provides historic background information about the earliest form of true RVing, namely, auto camping. $75-100.

Vintage RV Book. Standard hard-cover book, text and black & white photos, 5.5" x 8.5", by Wally Byam & David McKay Company, 303 pages, copyright 1960. Title: *Trailer Travel Here And Abroad*. This scarce book is simply an enjoyable one to read, especially as it chronicles some of the very early international trailer travels of Wally Byam. Just about each of the Airstream caravans described represented the first-ever travel trailer caravan to the part of the world that was traveled. Thus, it is a deeply valuable piece of RVing history. It's the perfect kind of book—one that you want to keep reading to its end, without having to put it down. $50-100.

recent years the number of auto campers has mounted well up into the millions…. There are approximately 4,000 cities and towns in the United States offering some accommodations to motor campers." That was more than eighty-five years ago!

Wally Byam was very smart and so savvy. He could have easily built trailers like those being produced by everyone else, and he could have sat back and hoped the sheer level of demand would have sustained his business. But, not Wally Byam. He built Airstream. It stands out, and it's outstanding. He certainly did not have to go globetrotting in a travel trailer to remote places when it had never been done before and when it was extremely difficult and dangerous. He did not have to write two RV books (that have become classic, almost required, RV reading), and he did not have to lead Airstream caravans and promote Airstream parks and rallies, and on and on. But he did, and the legacy of his business ethic has survived. The result is that the loyalty of Airstream owners and the dependability and stylishness of Airstream trailers have sustained the company longer than any other RV manufacturer. We hope you will agree that Airstream deserves to have at least one more book illustrate its many qualities and its interesting past.

In the coming pages, you will see over 370 pictures of more than 425 different pieces of Airstream memorabilia in our effort to tell some of the Airstream story, including some 285 postcards. We have also included family photos, medallions, toys, magazine covers, advertisements, artwork, and much more. In our attempt to be most helpful to our readers, we have included a descriptive caption for every piece of Airstream memorabilia shown in the book, along with an estimated value for each item. We have done our best to provide accurate information, but we readily admit that full information about some vintage pieces may not be available (so, for instance, we have had to estimate the ages of certain pieces, and we have disclosed when we have made such estimations).

For each item, we have indicated the material with which it is constructed, the type of image (such as a real photo or a graphic design), its size, its maker, its serial number (if any), its age, its estimated value, and possibly other details (such as, for postcards, whether it was used or is unused). About the estimated values, this book is intended to serve as a price guide, not as the gospel on valuation. Hence, we have provided a range of values for each item. Reasonable minds may differ somewhat about a matter as subjective as price or value, especially when—as is always the case with regard to collectibles—condition is extremely relevant. Importantly, when affixing our prices, we have attempted to estimate the value of each piece to a serious collector or purchaser of such an item.

In conclusion, we want to extend our most sincere thanks to Rich Luhr, the Editor of *AIRSTREAM LIFE*, the celebrated and leading Airstream publication, for his generous and thoughtful Foreword to this book. He is a walking encyclopedia about Airstream and, of course, one of the leading authorities on everything Airstream. We are pleased to count him as a friend and colleague among those who admire, study, and write about Airstream.

Anniversary Lapel Pin. Lightweight metal & hard plastic, circular crest with stick pin & clasp, two-color graphics, 1" diameter, by Airstream, unnumbered, dated 2006. Inscription: "Airstream 75 Anniversary 1931-2006." No other RV manufacturer has had the opportunity to celebrate its 75th anniversary. $10-15.

Chapter 1

AIRSTREAM Background

Before Airstream was created in the early 1930s, many cultural and technological events and trends had come together to lay the foundation for Airstream's successful history. And, Wally Byam was certainly aware of them. This chapter will showcase some of the most important of those factors—although there simply is not enough time and space here to tell the full story leading up to the development of Airstream. Yet, a basic understanding of these matters will be useful, for there are several common threads from this background information that will be apparent throughout the rest of this book.

The most significant background factors to note are: (1) the many vehicle "roll" models that would influence the invention of travel trailers; (2) the birth of the automobile and the rapid advent of auto camping; (3) the art deco movement and the resulting streamline influence on design; and, (4) the creation of a vast array of boxy travel trailer brands, all of which looked basically alike. Out of this mix, Wally Byam and Airstream burst onto the scene and have reigned supreme, for 80+ years.

In hindsight, there could have been no doubt that the travel trailer would be created, because (even before the automobile was invented) there were so many models of wheeled vehicles suggesting the prospect of a recreational trailer that would transport passengers, would serve as a carrier of clothing, food, and supplies, and would provide enclosed sleeping quarters for extended travel. These vehicles included many types of horse-drawn carriages [such as the gypsy wagon, the circus wagon, the covered wagon, the church wagon, and others]. Also included were railroad passenger cars [especially those with trolley-style roof designs and those used as camping cars (which could be pulled onto sidings and used by wealthy patrons for overnight stays in outdoor settings)].

Advertising Postcard. Unused, real black & white photo, 5.75" x 3.5", by Airstream, unnumbered, c. 1950s. This original postcard contained one of the all-time classic Airstream publicity shots—highlighting Airstream's Commodore model. The picture has appeared many times in Airstream literature. The card bears the Airstream address in Los Angeles, rather than the Jackson Center location. The text on the back reads: "This latest trailer of Cornelius Vanderbilt Jr. and Wally Byam, world-famous globe trotters is more modern than a space ship and contains about everything including the first astrodome in a trailer. The Commodore will be at the Chicago political conventions and after at the London Coronation of Queen Elizabeth." On the side of the trailer was the caption: "World Traveling Land Liner," along with the list of cities it had visited. Airstream's publicity efforts were far superior to any of its competitors. $50-75.

The trolley style roofs featured on a number of the pictured horse-drawn wagons and on train carriages and streetcars has a significance for travel trailer design. Of course, the trolley roof runs down the center of a wagon or coach and, thereby, provides added headroom where it is needed in the area where people stand and walk in those vehicles. Numerous early box-shaped American, and especially British, travel trailers were made with trolley roofs. But, Airstream did not need to adopt this feature because Airstream's rounded bullet shape, including its curved roof and ceiling, provides additional headroom down the middle of the trailer.

Of course, the invention of the automobile was necessary to provide the power source to effectively pull travel trailers. But, immediately [and even before travel trailers were created] there developed a great interest in auto camping. The car allowed people much further access to the outdoors and to camping than they previously enjoyed. People could go farther into the countryside in a much shorter time than before. Thus, tourist courts and parks and campgrounds began to spring up to meet the demands of the new generation of wanderers. Camping organizations and camping publications got their starts in the 1920s. For example, the Tin Can Tourists group originated in 1919 and is still quite active today.

Advertising Postcard. Unused, real color photo, 6" x 4", by Douglas Keister & Gibbs Smith Publisher, c. 2004. Caption: "RVTV." This card promotes the RVTV program "A Contemporary View of the Open Road." This spectacular contemporarily staged scene of a 1934 Packard Roadster towing a 1935 Bowlus Papoose trailer is from our friend Doug Keister's outstanding 2004 book *SILVER PALACES*. It should be in your RV library. For more of his great RV books, see our bibliography or go to keisterphoto.com. You can readily see how Bowlus was the true predecessor to Airstream. $10-15.

Greeting Card. Standard greeting card paper, bi-fold, real black & white photo, 5.5" x 4.25" folded [5.5" x 8.5" unfolded], by MikWright Ltd [mikwright.com], c. 2000s. Greeting inside card: "Meet Sven and Olga, The Original Happy Campers." This fun and nostalgic picture showed a 1930s aluminum trailer, with its classic rounded rear panels and its straight-faced owners posing beside it. The clever MikWright philosophy for their unique cards is to produce "greetings that push buttons, poke fun, and provoke something." This card succeeds in each of those ways. $10-15.

The period of the 1920s-40s was the peak of the era of the art deco movement with its avant-garde designs and with particular attention focused upon streamline design in transportation [such as in the construction of locomotives, steamships, automobiles, and airplanes]. Color was important too, as revealed by the creative and dramatic novelty of colors and their pastel shades (which we now call retro).

However, even in the era of art deco, the hundreds of companies in the fledgling travel trailer industry seemed to center their attention upon the shoebox design of trailers, largely with dull exterior colors, with weighty construction materials, and with little creativity. Perhaps,

that mentality was understandable in a new industry still coping with basic concerns about building roadworthy and dependable coaches, and fearing survival because so many competitors were in the trailer marketplace.

Even in the 1930s, the airplane was a new and exciting phenomenon for most of the population, because they had never flown in a plane. And, airplanes were sleek and shiny and modern. Commercial aviation for the masses was decades away. Owning an airplane was unattainable and unimaginable for almost everyone, but owning an Airstream with its airplane fuselage design and its bright airplane aluminum surface was possible.

AIRSTREAM
right for the cars of the thirties –
right for the cars of the seventies.

Publicity Brochure [underneath]. Standard brochure covers & paper, real color photo, 8" x 11", by Airstream, 1978. Caption: "Airstream—Pioneer of the lightweight aerodynamic trailer." This photo is an example of just one page from the annual brochure called *The Airstream Story*. This picture-perfect view of a 1930s sedan and Airstream trailer actually appeared twice in 1978's brochure. The image and caption here appeared in the second picture near the end of the brochure and captured the essence of what Airstream did to distinguish itself from the other trailer manufacturers, as we will see in the coming pages of this introductory chapter. In the first version of this photo early in the brochure, the caption reads: "Airstream – Right for the cars of the thirties – Right for the cars of the seventies." These annual brochures included not only the history of Airstream (including numerous vintage photographs), but also illustrated the current line of Airstream coaches, and the earlier ones have become highly sought-after. For the brochure, $50-75.

Christmas Ornament [on top]. Standard lightweight ornament, glass, silver & black graphics, 5.5" x 2.25" x 3.25", by Jennifer Ellsworth Landmarks, 2003. Fantastic upscale Christmas collectible! This spectacular replica of a 1936 Airstream Clipper was produced in Poland, where it was hand-blown and hand-painted. Note the realistic details—tandem axles, curved front and rear roof panels, side entry door, and shiny exterior finish. It looks so much like several of the other images. $50-75.

Wally Byam was savvy enough to avoid following the pack of other trailer makers, and smart enough to look for something unique to market to the American public. He settled upon Airstream. Airstream's streamline bullet design was different; Airstream's shiny silver aluminum appearance was different; Airstream's name was different [combining the notions of air flowing around a streamline design]; and, Airstream's future publicity and advertising campaigns were going to be vastly bigger, spectacularly better, and uniquely different from those of any of its competitors. In this publicity department, Airstream was destined to be far ahead of its time and light-years ahead of its competition.

For the record, mention should be made of the fact that Airstream did manufacture motorhomes for several extended periods of time, and that those RVs were generally well-liked by their owners. However, motorhomes are significantly different creatures than travel trailers, and Airstream simply could not do the same innovative and unique kinds of things with its motor coaches that it had so successfully done with its trailers. Airstream eventually discontinued its production of motorhomes, although it continues to produce a popular camper van, called the Airstream Interstate.

Historical Postcard. Unused, chrome, 5.5" x 3.5", by Dexter Press, unnumbered, c. 1970s. Caption: "Early Day Mobile Homes." This vintage card shows the old painting entitled *Yoking Up In Corral* by William H. Jackson, which he first sketched in 1866 and which is housed in the collection of the Nebraska State Historical Society in Lincoln, Nebraska. The covered wagons in the corral are, of course, the "early day mobile homes," and the covered wagon continues to be one of the most important early roll models for the travel trailer, as the other images will exemplify. $5-10.

Magazine Advertisement. Standard magazine paper, black & white graphics, 4" x 5.75", by Covered Wagon Company, in *LIFE*, April 12, 1937, page 87. This actual advertising piece illustrated one of the models of Covered Wagon trailer homes. Covered Wagon borrowed its name from those early vehicles of western wagon train fame and became one of the most popular brands of its time. But, notice the trailer's boxy shape that became the common design among the trailers of the 1930s-50s. $10-15.

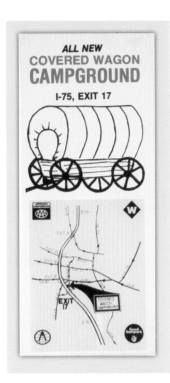

Advertising Postcard. Unused, tri-color graphics, rectangular 3.75" x 8.5", no maker, unnumbered, c. 1980s. This advertising card for Covered Wagon Campground in Tifton, Georgia, boasted in the text on the back that it had 55 pull thru spaces and was located "just 90 minutes drive away from Plains, Georgia." This park also took its name from the familiar view of covered wagons as early forms of mobile homes or travel trailers. The comparison of covered wagons to modern travel trailers was so commonplace that even Wally Byam used it in his 1960 book *Trailer Travel Here And Abroad*. He wrote as the caption for a picture of a family while eating breakfast along the route of the old Oregon Trail and while inside their Airstream trailer (showing its traditional curved ceiling): "Covered wagon, twentieth-century style…" $5-10.

English Tourist Postcard. Used, real photo, 5.5" x 3.5", no maker, #20383, posted 1904. Caption: "Bohemians." This old card bears an English stamp and postmark, and was sent to an address in Britain. The gypsy wagon is thought by many to be the earliest close ancestor to the travel trailer, because those "Bohemians" traveled in it, carried their belongings in it, slept in it, and ate in it (depending upon conditions outside)—which describes how we use modern travel trailers. Ted Lyons in his interesting and informative article "You Can Take It With You" in *COAST TO COAST*, Sept.-Oct. 1992 wrote: "It is the Gypsies, more than any other group, whose name conjures up images of travel—and trailers." $20-25.

Japanese Tourist Postcard. Unused, real black & white photo, 5.5" x 3.5", c. 1900-1910. This remarkable picture showed a tall and sizable royal or ceremonial wagon supported by two large wheels and pulled by at least four horses (and perhaps some of the men in attendance). A total of some fifteen characters written in Japanese appeared on the front and back of the card. On the reverse side were the words "Post Card, Carte Postale, and Postkarte," with only a very small 1.75" wide area on the left side available for the sender to write a message. $30-40.

English or Canadian Tourist Postcard. Unused, real black & white photo, 5.5" x 3.5", no maker, unnumbered, c. 1900. Caption: "On The Road Touring England & Canada." The large carriage in the middle of this scene appeared distinctly upscale in comparison to the gypsy wagon of the preceding card, and looked like a private trolley car with its trolley-style roof line and windows. This coach could certainly have carried passengers, provided storage, and included sleeping quarters. $20-25.

Dutch Tourist Postcard. Unused, real black & white photo, 5.5" x 3.5", by Vivat of Amsterdam, #3072, c. 1890s-1900s. Exceptional find! Caption: "Scheveningen" [a Dutch city with a large beach front nearby]. Interestingly, the printed instructions on the back of this card are written in both Dutch and French. This tourist postcard showed the remarkable picture of two fantastic, early, mobile, miniature beach or bath "houses"—demonstrating the wide variety of wheeled vehicles that preceded travel trailers and that cumulatively influenced the development of modern trailers. Obviously, if people had the ingenuity to think of this beach trailer design, once the car was invented, what would people be expected to create to pull behind it? $50-75.

English Tourist Postcard. Unused, real black & white photo, 5.5" x 3.5", no maker, #539, c. 1890-1900. Remarkable image! This Church Army caravan was a horse-drawn wooden wagon, and it had a number of features of the travel trailers that were to follow along over the next 30-40 years—such as a trolley-style roof with windows that could be opened, coach windows with shutters that could be raised or lowered and with curtains inside, a storage box or area under the rear of the wagon, and a stove with a smoke stack protruding up through the roof. Notice that there was also a curved roof over the driver's area to protect the driver from the elements and a curtain that could be pulled closed to shelter the entry area. $40-50.

Tourist Postcard. Unused, real black & white photo, 5.5" x 3.5", by Kruxo, unnumbered, c. 1890-1910. Yahoo! This rare card showed a simple box-shaped horse-drawn work wagon, made primarily of canvas or thin wood, which apparently was used by range hands or telegraph linemen. Two workers were shown seated on a blanket for a meal served on a makeshift table. The wagon could have been used for several purposes – including transporting the workers, their equipment and food, and sleeping gear. Some of the earliest travel trailers were made largely of canvas roofs and/or sides, and many were made principally of wood. $30-40.

Tourist Postcard. Unused, real black & white photo, 5.5" x 3.5", no maker, unnumbered, c. 1900-1920. Fantastic picture! This card showed what might be one of the earliest true mobile homes. It appeared to be the housing used by an extended family of migrant farm workers in North Dakota [where the picture was taken, according to a handwritten note on the back]. Built in a shoebox shape, this wooden structure rested upon four metal wagon wheels, and it had windows, a sliding door, and a stove with stovepipe vented through the roof. We do not know how many of the 12 people pictured here would have resided in this mobile housing. $40-50.

English Tourist Postcard. Used, real black & white photo, 5.5" x 3.5", by Paget Prize [Self Toning], unnumbered, posted 1903. Incredible! This trolley car in the woods is an actual recreational vehicle! These sporty camping fellows enjoyed an upscale version of mobile housing much better than that shown on the preceding card. This early British RV was probably a miniature weekend country get-a-way, complete with trolley roof with small opening windows, a neatly capped stove pipe vented through the roof, pristine window curtains with tie-backs inside, shutters outside, and even a ladder to the roof [undoubtedly for sunbathing]. Stamped in, and sent to, England. This horse-drawn coach looked just like a train carriage, without the tracks, converted to camping use. But, compare with the next two cards. $50-75.

Advertising Postcard. Unused, real black & white photo, 5.5" x 3.5", by L.M.S., unnumbered, c. 1920s-50s. Caption: "An LMS Holiday Caravan." It was really an RV, showing more details than the previous card. Notice this British card illustrated the fineries of the clothing of the passengers, who certainly would not be roughing it while "camping." Indeed, some of these ladies were undoubtedly the maids or attendants. $30-40.

Advertising Postcard. Unused, real black & white photo, 5.5" x 3.5", by L.N.E.R., unnumbered, c. 1920s-50s. Caption: "L.N.E.R. Camping Coach." Another genuine recreational vehicle! This British card promoted the railway camping carriage, which could be stopped along the tracks for sightseeing or parked on a railroad siding overnight for eating and sleeping, and which was used by wealthy passengers. The text on the back read: "L.N.E.R. Camping Coaches accommodate six persons and are equipped with every requisite for a camping holiday. The rent is [300 pounds] per week. Details from any L.N.E.R. Station or Office." $30-40.

Magazine Advertisement. Standard magazine paper, real black & white photo, 8" x 11", by Star Cars, in *LITERARY DIGEST*, July 11, 1925, page 41. Caption: "Low-Cost Transportation ... Star Cars." This original automobile advertisement actually promoted auto camping, for it showed a family happily tent camping with their car, and its text began with the question: "Why not spend your vacation on a delightful, healthful auto-camping trip?" The ad even noted what we have already said, that the automobile allowed people to more readily "reach America's mountains, seashores, forests and lakes." Even at such an early date, the advertisement noted the availability of "thousands of municipal campsites," and this number was only one facet of the beginning of the dramatic explosion of auto camping and of American campgrounds. The prices for the various models of the new Star Cars appeared in small print and ranged between $540 and $820. $20-25.

Publicity Postcard. Used, real black & white photo, 5.5" x 3.5", no maker, unnumbered, posted 1920. This rare card was a publicity piece for a fellow named Arthur Jones, and its border caption read: "See America first. Covered 41 states. Four years on the road. Camped every night. Arthur Jones." Amazing! Notice how the car became part of a tent structure when a canvass section was attached to the passenger side of the auto. $40-50.

Publicity Postcard. Used, chrome, 5.5" x 3.5", by Florida News Co. & C.T. American Art, unnumbered, posted 1925. Caption: "Tin Can Tourist Camp, De Soto Park, Tampa, Fla." As auto camping was getting its real start, so was the Tin Can Tourists [TCT] organization. In fact, the official TCT group began its life in 1919 in De Soto Park in Tampa, which was the very camp shown on this card. Interestingly, the camper's handwritten message on the back of this card said: "We have been in camps where there are as many as 250 to 300 cars at a time." The TCT group actually served as an important influence contributing to the burgeoning popularity of auto camping and RVing. $10-15.

Tourist Postcard. Used, real black & white photo, 5.5" x 3.5", no maker, unnumbered, posted 1921. This rare old card showed how some creative early auto campers modified their vehicles to accommodate camping. This vehicle had a sleeping and storage area built upon it. Notice the foldout rear section with its support post and the opening side section with a wooden shutter that could be raised and lowered. The senders' handwritten message on the front and back said: "We hope you will come & camp with us again next year. We went as far as York Beach [Maine]. Our outfit [presumably, their auto camper] was a success. It didn't rain so we couldn't test it in a storm." The postcard was sent from Connecticut to Vermont. $50-75.

Tourist Postcard. Used, chrome, 5.5" x 3.5", no maker, unnumbered, posted 1925. Caption: "Us Tin-Canners, Florida." This card was mailed in January [winter] of 1925 from a traveler visiting in Florida to a friend in Indiana. The sender's message on the back of the card commented: "I love this climate." The seasonal weather differences across the country were also key influences on auto camping and RVing. $10-15.

Auto-Camping Magazine [underneath]. Standard magazine cover & paper, multi-color graphic, 8.5" x 11.75", *MOTOR CAMPER & TOURIST*, Vol. 3, Sept. 1926, 226 pages. The image shown here was on the front cover. Interestingly, the combination of camping and the earliest forms of RVing had gained such a strong foothold that this magazine devoted to auto camping had originated in 1924. Note that the purchase price of this issue in 1926 was 25 cents. Today, for the complete issue, $50-75.

Publicity Postcard [on top]. Unused, chrome, 5.5" x 3.5", by Ashville Post Card & C.T. American Art, #126 & #105351, c. 1920s. Caption: "A 'Tin Can' Tourist Camp In Dixieland." TCT still exists, and the authors are proud members. $10-15.

Advertising Postcard. Unused, linen, 5.5" x 3.5", by Curteich, #1B-H469, c. 1940s. This very hard-to-find card advertised the travel trailers for Main-Line Trailer Company of Los Angeles, California. The company slogan on the back of the card read: "America's Greatest Value." Notice that the design of the trailers illustrated on this page and the next page tend to be quite boxy and plain, and there was not much creativity in this advertising either. Airstream changed all that. $25-50.

Advertising Postcard. Used, black & white graphics, 5.5" x 3.5", no maker, #634, posted 1934. Caption: " 'Silver Dome' – America's Outstanding Coach Value." This travel trailer advertising card is so rare and so classic that it is "outstanding," too. The postcard provided a wealth of information, including prices for the various models ranging from $495 to $1495. The back of the card even urged prospective buyers to attend the Chicago World's Fair to see the Silver Dome on display there. $75-100.

Advertising Postcard. Unused, linen, 5.5" x 3.5", no maker, #10,303, c. 1940s. Caption [in small, dark, barely readable print on the front bottom of the card]: "Compliments of Alma Trailer Co., Alma, Michigan." Presumably, this now-difficult-to-obtain card was intended to be simple and sophisticated. But, it contained no other print at all; it was not creative and catchy; its colors were dark and dull; and it simply did not rival what Airstream did with its coaches and its advertising, although the Alma brand was a fine quality trailer. $40-60.

Advertising Brochure. Standard brochure paper, real black & white photos, two-sided tri-fold design, 6" x 4" folded [6" x 11" unfolded], unnumbered, c. 1930s. Title: *The Wanderer Trailer*. This rare original brochure touted the Wanderer, measuring 14'6" long by 6'4" wide, costing $695, and manufactured in Los Angeles, California. Notice the slimp wheel or pivot wheel under the arm of the trailer hitch, and the very slightly-raised trolley–style roof. $25-50.

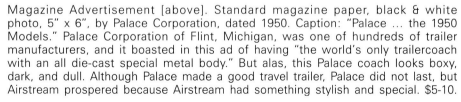

Magazine Advertisement [above]. Standard magazine paper, black & white photo, 5" x 6", by Palace Corporation, dated 1950. Caption: "Palace ... the 1950 Models." Palace Corporation of Flint, Michigan, was one of hundreds of trailer manufacturers, and it boasted in this ad of having "the world's only trailercoach with an all die-cast special metal body." But alas, this Palace coach looks boxy, dark, and dull. Although Palace made a good travel trailer, Palace did not last, but Airstream prospered because Airstream had something stylish and special. $5-10.

Advertising Postcard [below]. Used, real black & white photo, 5.5" x 3.5", by Willens & Company, #48141 [handwritten on front], dated & posted 1950. Caption: "Ringbolt Cabins & Trailer Park ... Hingham, Mass." According to the handwritten message on the back of this card, it was sent by the couple whose trailer is setting just right of center in the picture, with the flag flying behind it. The postcard was sent in late October from the park in Massachusetts to Sao Paulo, Brazil, with the couple's comment, "expect to leave for Florida soon." The trailers in the photo appeared to lack real luster, in contrast to the high spirit of Airstreams. $30-40.

Collector Postcard. Unused, real black & white photo, 4.25" x 6", by Joe Steinmetz Studio & Fotofolio, #A57, copyright 1982. Caption [on reverse side]: "Bradenton, Florida, 1951." So, this wonderful thirty-year-old card pictured a thirty-year-old trailer. The text on the back of the postcard pointed out that the picture was from "The Photography Archive, Carpenter Center For The Visual Arts, Harvard University." We are delighted that RVing is represented in the Harvard collection. $15-20.

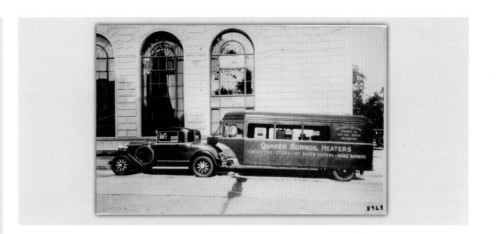

Advertising Postcard. Used, real black & white photo, 5.5" x 3.5", no maker, #8925 [handwritten on front], posted 1931. Caption: "Quaker Burnoil Heaters." This scarce card was probably made by the Preferred Utilities Company (whose name appears on the side of the coach) as a promotional postcard, because the handwritten message on its reverse side was sent to the Oil Heating Equipment Company of Groton, Connecticut. The message: "This rig will be turned over to use at New London [Connecticut] R.R. Station this Sunday at 1 P.M." Although Wally Byam might have chosen to produce 5th wheel RVs like the coach pictured here, thankfully, he opted for Airstream. See the 5th wheel coach on the next card as well. $25-50.

Magazine Advertisement [above]. Standard magazine paper, black & white photos, 5" x 6.5", by "M" System Manufacturing Company, c. 1950. Caption: "No reservations necessary … just pick up and go." The Deluxe Tandem model coach and its maker "M" System Manufacturing of Vicksburg, Mississippi, did not last long among all the competitors in the huge travel trailer marketplace. The coach here looked basically like so many others, but Airstream was different, stylish, and unique. $5-10.

Tourist Postcard [below]. Unused, real black & white photo, 5.5" x 3.5", no maker, unnumbered, c. 1940s. Notice the lady opening the door of the boxy travel trailer in the picture on this rare and spectacular card. $40-50.

Tourist Postcard. Unused, real black & white photo, 5.5" x 3.5", no maker, unnumbered, dated 1936. Caption: "Chittenden … Chapin … 10 Central Park West, N.Y.C. … Columbus 5-3587." This stunning card showed, in a classically staged setting, a perfectly matched pairing of a tow car (possibly a 1935 Oldsmobile) and a 5th wheel travel trailer. Airstream has never made a 5th wheel coach. It stands alone today as the maker of lightweight, aerodynamic, shiny-aluminum trailers. $50-75.

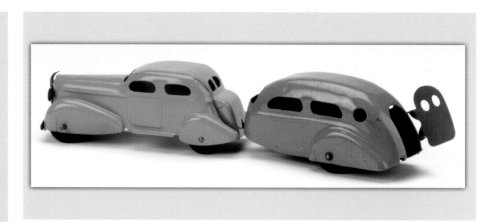

RV Toy Set. Restored pressed steel car & travel trailer pair, car measures 5.5" x 2" x 2" & trailer is 5" x 2" x 2", by Wyandotte Toys of Michigan, unnumbered, c. late 1930s. This quite colorful and outstanding toy set, made by a leading toy manufacturer of the time, incorporated two important features into its toy trailer which were similar to some of the actual early Bowlus and Airstream travel trailers—namely, a rear entry door, and a rounded/streamlined design. $100-150.

Magazine Advertisement. Standard magazine paper, full-page, black & white graphics, large 10" x 14", by Pan American World Airways, dated 1944. Caption: "Now you can fly to Alaska." This World War II ad for Pan American and its Alaska Clippers announced resumption of commercial flights to several cities in Alaska. Note the streamline design, aluminum construction and aerodynamic shape of the aircraft. This time period was part of the art deco era, and Airstream was in touch with the times—yet wanting to be different from others in the trailer industry. $15-20.

Publicity Postcard. Unused, real black & white photo [with colored sky added], 5.5" x 3.5", by E.C. Kropp, #M-799, c. 1930s-40s. Caption: "Fly in the new Ryan Brougham, sister-ship of Lindy's 'Spirit of St. Louis' ... Flying daily over Washington from the Washington Airport." This most unusual postcard promoted Washington Airport in the District of Columbia, which the card announced could be reached by streetcar for the fare of eight cents. Notice the plane's aerodynamic, aluminum-paneled fuselage—advantageous attributes borrowed by Airstream trailers. $20-25.

Collector Postcard. Unused, real color photo, 6" x 4.25", by Airstream & Chronicle Books, unnumbered, copyright 2000. Caption: "Airstream Factory, 1965." This card was one of those in the collector set of forty reproduction photos from Airstream's illustrious history. Here, two factory workers lifted the shell of an Airstream to make the point that it was aerodynamic, stylish, and especially lightweight. Airstream was not like the incredible hulks displayed in the adjacent advertisement. $5-10.

Collector Postcard. Unused, real color photo, 6" x 4.25", by Airstream & Chronicle Books, unnumbered, copyright 2000. Caption: "Airstream Factory." Like the adjacent postcard, the image on this card dates probably to the 1960s and made the point that Airstream trailers were not only lightweight, but also strong and dependable. $5-10.

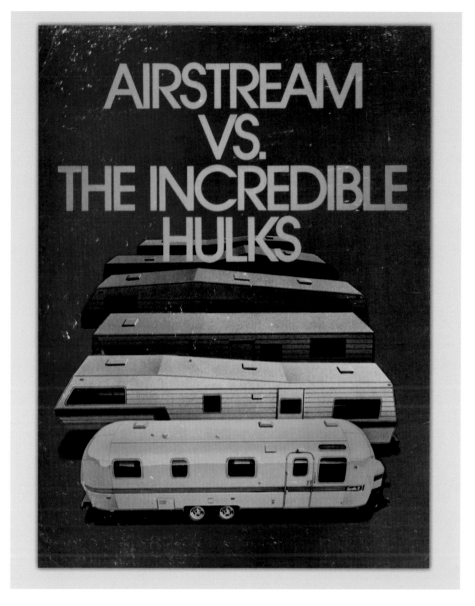

Magazine Advertisement. Standard magazine cover paper, multi-color graphics, full-page, 8" x 11", by Airstream, in *TRAILER LIFE*, May 1980 [inside front cover]. Caption: "Airstream vs. The Incredible Hulks." Outstanding imagery and message! This ad captured the most fundamental reason why Airstream has been so highly successful. Airstream is different from its competitors (and not just in its product, but in its publicity and advertising as well). $15-20.

Christmas Ornament. Standard ornament hand-blown glass, hand-painted black & silver graphics, 4.75" x 2.25" x 3.25", by Jennifer Ellsworth Landmarks, unnumbered, 2004. This amazing replica of a vintage coach illustrated an early Airstream in the collection of the Henry Ford Museum and Greenfield Village. Its details included the thirteen curved front and rear roof panels, the door-within-a-door design of many early Airstream side entry doors [on the other side of the trailer], and the Airstream name on the rear of the trailer. This fine ornament was produced in Poland. $50-75.

Magazine Article [underneath]. Standard magazine paper, real color photos, 8" x 10.5", entitled "Rare Air," in *FAMILY MOTOR COACHING*, March 2011, pages 54-57. Subtitle: "A First-Time Motorhome Owner Discovers That He's Acquired A Piece Of History." Family Motor Coach Association produces the leading RV publication *FAMILY MOTOR COACHING*, and it regularly contains interesting and valuable pieces about RVing history. This fascinating article tells the story of an RVer who bought and restored a rare 1989 Airstream 370 LE "silver bullet" style motorhome. This model was the longest classic aluminum design motorhome that Airstream made, and the 370 LE was in production for just one year with only fifteen coaches completed. The new owner obtained a vanity license plate for his classic coach which read: "RAREAIR" [hence, the title of this article]. For the article, $5-10.

Advertising Postcard. Unused, real color photo, 6" x 4", by Viking Studio Books, unnumbered, 2003. Caption: *"Ready To Roll ... A Celebration of the Classic American Travel Trailer ... Arrol Gellner and Douglas Keister."* This card promoted the marvelous RV book *Ready To Roll* by Arrol Gellner and our friend Doug Keister. This book is a fun and valuable resource with text and 300 pictures that should be on the self of every RV enthusiast. And, with so many trailers from which to choose for their book's cover image, Gellner and Keister selected a vintage Airstream! Doug Keister has authored a number of RV books. See our bibliography, or go online to keisterphoto.com. For the postcard, $15-20.

Advertising Postcard [on top]. Used, real color photograph, 6" x 4", by Airstream, unnumbered, posted 2003. Caption: "Airstream 390 Series." The front and back of this card advertised Airstream diesel motorhomes, and the card was sent from Airstream's headquarters in Jackson Center, Ohio, on behalf of an Airstream dealer in Colorado to a prospective purchaser in Colorado. Of course, the design for these diesel motorhomes adopted the standard box shape, rather than the earlier Airstream bullet coaches. There were not too many advertising postcards produced for Airstream motorhomes. $10-15.

Chapter 2

AIRSTREAM Advertising

Several reasons explain why the Airstream travel trailer became a true American icon. Among them are the design features of Airstream trailers, which have elements that make them stand above all others as unique and memorable—including Airstream's shiny aluminum exterior and its airplane fuselage shape. And, equally significant are both the construction and quality control, reasons for Airstream's dependability and longevity.

Yet, Airstream could not have achieved nearly as high a place in RVing without its aggressive and masterful publicity efforts over the last 80+ years. Indeed, those publicity steps have made Airstream THE legendary American travel trailer. That advertising included a large number of picture postcards, brochures, and other publicity pieces produced by Airstream and by numerous other companies which included Airstreams in their ad campaigns.

The key elements of the publicity efforts initiated by Airstream's founder and publicity genius Wally Byam were (1) his thoughtful and compelling slogans to describe the allure and reality of owning an Airstream trailer, (2) his national and international caravans and rallies, and (3) his remarkably aggressive and effective advertising campaigns. We include two separate chapters later in the book in which we will look at Airstream rallies and international Airstream caravans.

This chapter examines Airstream's philosophy and slogans, and its advertising promotions. From almost its beginning, Wally Byam understood the value of a simple and memorable company philosophy, particularly if it were reduced to a series of clever and meaningful pictures and slogans that could be widely publicized. The images and catch phrases have stood the test of time, and remain as persuasive for Airstream today as they were decades ago. Most notably among the slogans is: "SEE MORE. DO MORE. LIVE MORE."

Many years ago, especially in the 1950s, Airstream mounted a most successful advertising campaign, the cornerstone of which was the effective photography done by Ardean Miller. The Miller family was going on Wally Byam's European caravan in 1956. Ardean's

JUST ARRIVED...BIG TRAILER LUXURY IN A SMALL PACKAGE!

Advertising Postcard. Used [bulk rate postmark], real black & white photo, large 7" x 5.25", by Airstream, unnumbered, c. 1960s. Caption: "Just Arrived ... Big Trailer Luxury In A Small Package!" This outstanding card was a classic example of Airstream techniques in effective publicity, and it was sent from Jackson Center, Ohio, to Glendale, California. Notice that the two Airstreams were hitched to luxury Lincoln and Mercedes automobiles. The small Bambi Airstream was intended as the real focus of this postcard and of the text on the front and back. The text made successful use of thoughtful slogans, a common thread of Airstream advertising. For example, on the back: "See it now ... Try it now ... Enjoy it now!" $40-50.

wife Norma was going to write a major article about the caravan for *National Geographic Magazine*, and professional photographer Ardean was to take the pictures for that article. Byam saw that Ardean was a very talented photographer and hired him for Airstream. The rest is history, because for the next twenty years Ardean took the thoughtful and memorable advertising and publicity photos that helped make Airstream a legend.

Importantly, Airstream was the beneficiary of a great deal of free publicity from the producers of other products and services, because other companies wanted to be positively associated with a product as trusted and successful as Airstream. Thus, campgrounds, insurance companies, auto and truck manufacturers, cigarette makers, and other corporations often included Airstream trailers in publicity photographs. Since Airstreams are so instantly recognizable, the exposure was invaluable to Airstream.

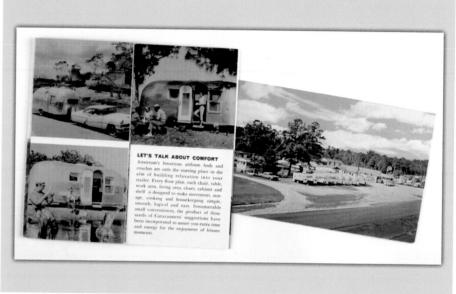

Advertising Brochure [left]. Folding [tri-fold – 12 panel] design, standard typing paper weight, color graphics & real black & white [colored] photos, small 2.75" x 5.25" folded [16.5" x 5.25" unfolded], by Airstream, unnumbered, c. 1962. Title: *Your Passport To Travel Adventure*. This rare piece touted the benefits provided by an Airstream for purposes of trailer traveling, even for going abroad. $20-25.

Advertising Postcard [right]. Unused, real color photo, 5.5" x 3.5", by R.A. Lasater, #81622, c. 1960s. This card promoted Indian River Trailer Sales in Cocoa, Florida, and more than a dozen Airstreams were visible on the sales lot. $10-15.

Advertising Brochure [left]. The same brochure shown with the two preceding postcards. Folded in this position, the brochure revealed three actual photographs, accompanied by a discussion of trailer comfort (namely, "Airstream's luxurious" amenities).

Advertising Postcard [right]. Unused, real color photo, 5.5" x 3.5", by Dexter Press & Habod Advertising Products, #17668-C, dated 1975. This text on the back of the card advertised a full service operation at Bell's Trailer Park in Tallahassee, Florida—including a trailer park, trailer sales, service station, grocery store, laundry, fishing lake, US Post Office, and "Wally Byam Store." Bell's sold Airstream and three other brands of travel trailers. Five Airstream trailers can be seen in the picture. $10-15.

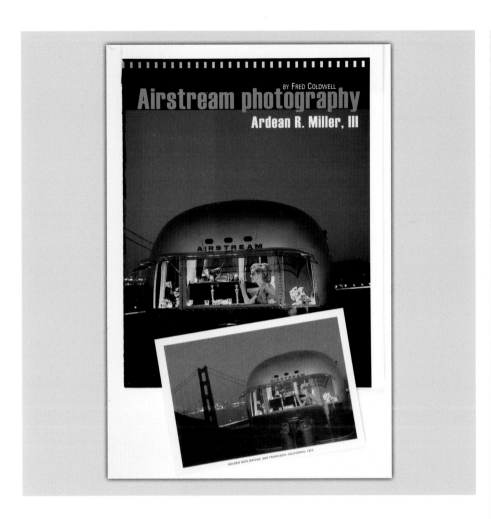

Magazine Article [underneath]. Standard magazine paper, real color photo, 8" x 11", in *AIRSTREAM LIFE*, by Fred Coldwell, "The Man Who Defined Airstream Photography: Ardean R. Miller III," Winter 2007. This fascinating article told the story of the photographer-genius Ardean Miller, and his methods. Wally Byam hired Miller in the 1950s to do the photography for Airstream—for the next twenty years from 1957-1976. The picture shown here is a portion of one of the many memorable Miller shots, in this case a night scene from 1972 of a sophisticated lady seated for a fine dinner in an Airstream parked with the Golden Gate Bridge in the background. The complete image appears on the adjacent postcard. For the article, $5-10.

Collectible Postcard [on top]. Unused, real color photo, 6" x 4.25", by Airstream & Chronicle Books, unnumbered, copyright 2000. This image shows the collectible postcard produced from the 1972 Ardean Miller photo appearing in the magazine article noted above. Airstream was vigilant about keeping original photographs and reusing them in various mediums for advertising and publicity purposes. This method was an especially sound business practice since so many of the Miller photos were outstanding and were, therefore, worthy of reuse. $5-10.

Advertising Brochure. Heavy weight brochure paper, black & white graphics, 8.5" x 11", by Chrysler-Plymouth, #81-505-1032, 8 pages, dated 1971. Title: *1971 Chrysler-Plymouth Trailer-Towing Packages*. Wonderful modern cover graphic! In keeping with the uphill climb being illustrated for the tow car and Airstream on the front of this striking booklet, the Chrysler-Plymouth slogan "Coming Through" was printed in the brochure's bottom right corner. The brochure also included another black & white illustration of an Airstream trailer being towed [on the inside front cover of the booklet]. A "winged" Shasta trailer was shown as well on page three of this handsome brochure. $25-50.

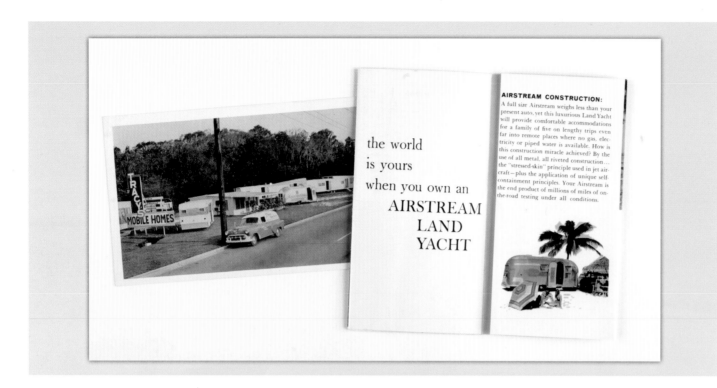

Advertising Postcard [left]. Unused, real black & white photo, 5.5" x 3.5", by Picto Cards, unnumbered, dated 1959. This rare card was produced for Tracy's Mobile Homes in Leesburg, Florida. The text on the back read: "Live enjoyably, live luxuriously, enjoy Florida living the mobile home way. ... Where quality tells and service sells." It is somewhat curious that the small Airstream trailer was setting on a mobile home lot along with much longer coaches. $30-40.

Advertising Brochure [right]. This image is taken from the same brochure shown with the previous postcard on page 24. Caption here: "The world is yours when you own an Airstream Land Yacht."

Advertising Brochure. Heavy weight paper, color graphics, quad-fold [8 panel], 9.5" x 4.5" folded [19" x 18" unfolded], by General Motors, unnumbered, dated 1966. Entitled: *Custom Tailor Your '66 Buick For Tuned Trailering*. Wow! A personal favorite. The vibrant colors used throughout this rare brochure make it a highly collectible piece, especially with the striking image on its front cover of a bright yellow Buick station wagon pulling a handsome Airstream. $30-40.

Advertising Brochure [underneath]. Standard brochure paper, real color photos, 8.75" x 11", by Airstream, unnumbered, 36 pages, copyright 1965. Title [on cover]: *The Airstream Story*. Although postcard images of Airstreams always show only the exteriors of the trailers, the expanded space of a multi-page brochure also allowed for room to illustrate the interior of Airstreams, as was most effectively shown here (on page 28) for the 1966 line of coaches. For the brochure, $50-75.

Collector Postcard [on top]. Unused, real black & white photo, 6" x 4.25", by Airstream & Chronicle Books, unnumbered, copyright 2000. This fun image from 1963 actually shows a lady applying her lipstick by looking at her reflection in the shiny aluminum finish of the Airstream trailer. Airstream's legendary slogan "Live more … See more … Do more" is printed in the bottom border of the card. You will see in the upcoming pages that the order of this slogan's three phrases have been rearranged from time to time. $5-10.

Advertising Brochure. Standard brochure paper, color graphics & real color photos, 8.5" x 11", by Jeep/Eagle, #3-2424-853-01, 12 pages, c. 1970s. Title: *Jeep/Eagle Technovation … 4-Wheel Drive Trailering*. The cover of this creatively designed brochure featured a high-tech graphic of a Jeep tow vehicle and an Airstream trailer. In addition, there was a real color photo of a Jeep pulling an Airstream trailer on the inside of the booklet, on page 4. $15-20.

TRAVEL IS PURE PLEASURE WHEN YOU GO IN AN AIRSTREAM

Advertising Postcard. Used, real black & white photo, large 7" x 5.25", by Airstream, unnumbered, c.1950s [posted, but no date stamp]. Caption: "Travel Is Pure Pleasure When You Go In An Airstream." Airstream used a lot of these large-scale cards. This impressive postcard was supplied to dealers for them to send to prospective buyers of trailers, and in this case the back of the postcard bears an ink-stamp for Langhurst Motor Company of Cedar Rapids, Iowa. The card was sent to a possible purchaser in nearby East Moline, Illinois. The Airstream company text on the reverse of the card seemed quite apropos for the scene captured in the picture on the card's front: "There is nothing to compare with the 'Airstream' way of life. Go where you like, stay as long as you please. You're as free as a bird on wing..." $40-50.

AIRSTREAM LAND YACHTING—THE BETTER WAY TO TRAVEL

Advertising Postcard. Unused, real color photo, large 7" x 5.25", by Airstream, unnumbered, c. 1960s. Caption: "Airstream Land Yachting—The Better Way To Travel." Ah! What a wonderful family portrait, showing mom, dad, and the kids all enjoying their day fishing in a country pond with their personal, shiny, self-contained Airstream house-on-wheels only a few feet away, providing conveniences, shelter, and security. $20-30.

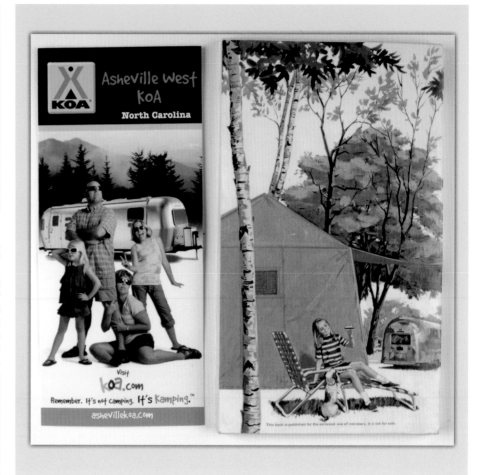

Advertising Rack Card [left]. Light-weight cardboard, real color photo & multi-color graphics, 4" x 9", by KOA, unnumbered, c. 2010. Caption: "Asheville West KOA ... North Carolina." Many individual KOA Kampgrounds produce and distribute these large rectangular promotional cards, each of which contains information on the front and back about the subject KOA. Such rack cards are not postcards, as they have no spaces for addresses, messages, or postage stamps. This handsome card showed a shiny Airstream as part of its backdrop for the pictured camping family. $5-10.

Campground Directory [right]. Back cover, standard brochure weight covers & pages, color graphics & black & white photos, 5.5" x 9.25", by American Automobile Association, 292 pages, copyright 1966. Title: *Western Campground Directory*. The scene depicted on the back cover of this booklet was similar in content and style to the famous works of Norman Rockwell—with the happy outdoor camping subject, complete with a young girl, her dog, and their Airstream trailer. Incidentally, this RVing scene was part of a larger picture that continued onto the front of the brochure, showing other family members engaged in preparing lunch. $20-25.

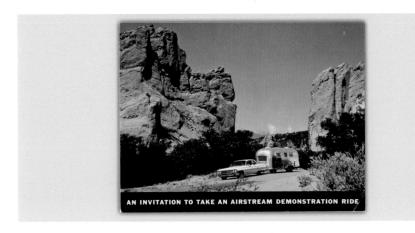

Advertising Postcard. Unused, real color photo, large 7" x 5.25", by Airstream, unnumbered, dated 1964. Caption: "An Invitation To Take An Airstream Demonstration Ride." What a great marketing idea! The claim made in the text on the back of this most captivating card was "that the 1964 Airstream is America's most advanced travel trailer." The strategy employed by this postcard was an effective one—to give customers the opportunity for a test drive of travel trailers, just as they expected when purchasing automobiles. As the text continued: "Take an Airstream out on the road; take it up hill, down hill, across the ruttiest roads you can find. … You don't need a car, you don't need a hitch. Your Airstream dealer has everything ready and waiting for you." $30-40.

Advertising Postcard. Unused, real color photo, 5.5" x 3.5", by H.S. Crocker Company, unnumbered, c. 1960s. Caption: "Robert Christ and Company … the best place in the world to buy a mobile home." And, the text on the reverse side claimed this dealership was the "world's largest mobile home dealer." This dealer was on the south side of Chicago, Illinois, and the postcard is a very desirable one, especially with the mobile home in the picture resting on top of the building and the four Airstream trailers setting out front. $30-40.

Advertising Postcard. Unused, real color photo, large 7" x 5.25", by Airstream, unnumbered, c. 1960s. Caption: "Airstream Land Yachting—The Better Way To Travel." This card presented another ideal travel scene—the family enjoying a sunny day at the beach, with their trusted Airstream nearby. This particular serene family image has appeared a number of times in Airstream publications. $20-25.

Collector Postcard. Unused, real black & white photo, 6" x 4.25", by Airstream & Chronicle Books, unnumbered, copyright 2000. Caption: "Singing Sands Mountain, Nevada, 1962." Airstream looks comfortable everywhere, even in the desert. $5-10.

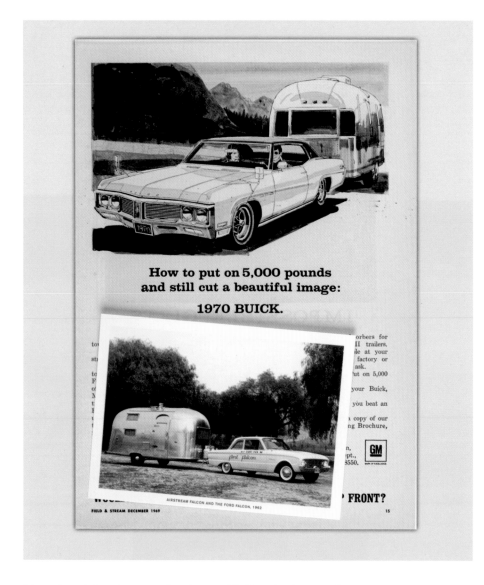

Magazine Advertisement [underneath]. Standard magazine paper, black & white graphic, 8.5" x 11", in *FIELD & STREAM*, December 1969. Caption: "How to put on 5,000 pounds and still cut a beautiful image: 1970 Buick." What a great tribute to Airstream, because the "beautiful image" was really a 1970 Buick towing an Airstream. $5-10.

Collector Postcard [on top]. Unused, real black & white photo, 6" x 4.25", by Airstream & Chronicle Books, unnumbered, copyright 2000. Caption: "Airstream Falcon and the Ford Falcon, 1962." Not surprisingly, as we have been seeing on these pages, the big automobile manufacturers all wanted their vehicles to be seen in the company of Airstream travel trailers, and Airstream got a lot of mileage from the associations as well. $5-10.

Magazine Article [underneath]. Standard magazine paper, real color photo, 8.25" x 11", in *AIRSTREAM LIFE*, Winter 2007, pages 46-47. The picture here fills one full page but is only about 2/3 of the entire picture appearing in this short two-page magazine piece entitled "From the Archives" and dedicated to the honor of Airstream's remarkable photographer Ardean Miller. The article called this scene "one of his magnificent color photographs. Taken in the early 1960s, this photo reveals why his Airstream photography is so compelling. " Later, the *AIRSTREAM LIFE* article so perceptively pointed out, "The appearance of an Airstream on the beach seems as natural as the girl's orange flippers. ... The young couple is the focal point of the photo, but by placing them in front of the Airstream, Ardean inevitably draws the viewer's eye to the trailer. ... Though obviously staged, nothing is out of place or incongruent." For the article, $5-10.

Collector Postcard [on top]. Unused, real color photo, 6" x 4.25", by Airstream & Chronicle Books, unnumbered, copyright 2000. Caption: "The World At Your Doorstep, 1960." Here is the complete picture. No wonder this photo was chosen to appear among the small group of 40 images in the Airstream collector postcard series. $5-10.

Advertising Postcard. Unused, real color tri-part photo, 5.5" x 3.5", by Advertising Services & Dexter Press, #75516-C, c. 1960s-70s. According to the text on the card's reverse side, the three photos on the front showed Jack & Patty Fast's Cascade Trailer Sales in Eugene, Oregon. The text also said: "Largest Airstream dealer in the Pacific Northwest. New and used Airstream travel trailers, complete service facilities, and Wally Byam accessory store." $15-20.

Advertising Postcard. Unused, real color 4-part photo, 5.5" x 3.5", by Waltz The Camera Man & Dexter Press, #68681-C, c. 1970s. The dealership promoted by this card was Avalon Travel Center in Canal Fulton, Ohio. A very close look at the pictures shows seven Airstreams outside and four inside the dealership. The text on the card's back proclaimed: "Ohio's largest Airstream and Vega dealer." $10-15.

Magazine Advertisement. Standard magazine paper, real black & white photo, 6" x 4.25", by Airstream, c. 1967. Caption: "Discover Real Travel Adventure." Both the photography and the language were effective in virtually every Airstream publicity piece. This beach scene contained all of the classic elements—the travelers, the palm trees, the water, the row boat, the lighthouse, and, of course, the Airstream. In keeping with the message of the caption, the text included some creative ideas, such as: "Perhaps you know a road somewhere you'd like to follow to the end," and "Follow your travel whims wherever they urge you to go." $5-10.

Advertising Postcard. Unused, real color tri-part photo, 6" x 4" with scalloped edges, by O'Brien Color Studios & Dexter Press, #37692-C, c. 1960s. Caption: "C.J. Stoll ... Mobile Homes ... Airstream." Interestingly, although the sign and caption spell "Airstream" as one word, the text on the reverse side of the card in two separate places spelled the name as "Air Stream"—two words. The pictures reveal some thirteen Airstream trailers on the sales lots, as C.J. Stoll had two sales facilities—one each in Bradenton and St. Petersburg, Florida. $10-15.

Magazine Advertisement [underneath]. Standard magazine paper, real color photo, 8" x 11", in *TRAILER LIFE*, May 1980. Caption: "Trailer owners from coast to coast agree … Modulator IV brake controller delivers superior braking performance!" Such a range of products are illustrated on the pages of this chapter, and the one common element is each manufacturer's desire to be associated with a trusted icon, Airstream. $5-10.

Magazine Advertisement [on top]. Standard magazine paper, real color photo, 8" x 5.5", in *TRAILER LIFE*, May 1980, page 28. Caption: "camp-a-float … your rv, our boat." Yahoo! What a clever idea—that never really quite caught on. Interestingly, the company CAF Industries was renting, but not selling, these flat-boat cruisers in five locations in five states—Arizona, Arkansas, California, Florida, and Oklahoma. Notice the Airstream sitting on the camp-a-float to the left side of the picture. $5-10.

Magazine Advertisement [underneath]. Standard magazine paper, real color photo, 7.25" x 10.5", c. 1960s. Caption: "Pall Mall Menthol 100's. Extra cool … extra mild." This scarce ad is one of our personal favorites because it employs simple, yet spectacular, imagery and it reminds us how times and perceptions change. Today, Airstream would not want to be linked to a cigarette ad. However, back in the 1960s, the Airstream situated at its serene forest campsite was part of the "extra cool" feeling that Pall Mall wanted to convey through this advertisement. $20-25.

Collector Ashtray [on top]. Clear glass, two-color graphic, 5" diameter with raised lip, and felt non-slip bottom, by Airstream, unnumbered, c. 1960s. Caption: "Airstream … Airstream trailers are guaranteed for life—your life! … Ask the man who tows one!" This piece is a great collectible because its graphic shows the classic Airstream image of the bicyclist towing an Airstream trailer, because it dates to those earlier days when smoking was more accepted, and because it is quite scarce. $40-50.

Collector Postcard. Unused, real black & white photo, 6" x 4.25", by Airstream & Chronicle Books, unnumbered, copyright 2000. Caption: "Another Happy Customer, 1959." Wow! Look at the mammoth length of this Airstream trailer. $5-10.

Advertising Postcard. Unused, real color photo, 6" x 4.25", by Airstream, unnumbered, c.1980s. Caption: "Airstream Classic Travel Trailer." This coach is a handsome lengthy trailer with three axles and six tires. Curiously, the photograph shows a man painting a picture of a lady standing next to the trailer, but the portrait on the easel does not include the Airstream in the background. Perhaps, although Ardean Miller did not take this photo, this composition is just as Miller would have wanted it. $10-15.

Collector Postcard. Unused, real black & white photo, 6" x 4.25", by Airstream & Chronicle Books, unnumbered, copyright 2000. Caption: "Family Holiday, 1962." Of course, the fostering of family values, especially the value of having the family travel together (in an Airstream travel trailer), was a central marketing theme. $5-10.

Advertising Postcard. Used, real color photo, 6" x 4.25", by Airstream, unnumbered, posted 1991. Caption: "Airstream ... 34' Limited 'Classic' Travel Trailer." Pictured is a long, long trailer with triple axles and the classy bullet look of Airstream! And interestingly, this particular card was printed on the reverse side with an invitation to attend Airstream's York, Pennsylvania, Buddy Rally from August 21-25, 1991. The card was sent from Jackson Center, Ohio, to a couple in Bristol, Pennsylvania. $10-15.

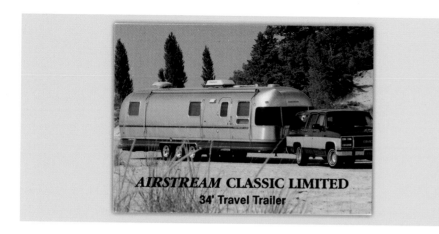

AIRSTREAM CLASSIC LIMITED
34' Travel Trailer

Advertising Postcard. Used, real color photo, 6" x 4.25", by Airstream, unnumbered, posted 1992. Caption: "Airstream Classic Limited ... 34' Travel Trailer." Here is an example of a postcard used to promote the parts and service department of a local Airstream dealer, Inland RV Service in Corona, California [as ink-stamped on the back of the card], because Inland was "exclusive owner of 1968 and prior Airstream parts." The postcard, however, was sent from Airstream headquarters in Jackson Center, Ohio, to a customer in Topanga, California. $10-15.

AIRSTREAM
CLASSIC
Rated "Best Buy" by Consumers Digest

Advertising Postcard. Used, real color photo, 6" x 4", by Airstream, unnumbered, posted 1994. Caption: "Airstream Classic ... Rated 'Best Buy' by Consumers Digest." The text on the back of this card announced, "the appointment of the newest Airstream dealer in the State of New York," which was Parrinello RV Center in Dansville, New York, and the card was sent to Airstream owners or prospective purchasers inviting them to visit a dealer and test drive an Airstream. The card concluded with this slogan: "Join in the Airstream way of camping." $10-15.

If you're pulling any of these, you may be killing your car.

AIRSTREAM SAFARI TRAVEL TRAILER

Magazine Advertisement [underneath]. Standard magazine paper, real color photo, 8" x 11", in *POPULAR SCIENCE*, dated 1970. Caption: "If you're pulling any of these, you may be killing your car." This ad for Travelall by International Harvester is clever and unique. The staged picture showed a vehicle apparently towing three trailers [uphill, too]—a boat and its trailer, a pop-up camper trailer, and an Airstream trailer. Then, in the very fine print at the bottom of the page appeared these words: "Situation depicted for demonstration purposes only." The ad pointed out that Travelall was "the one wagon built to tow up to five tons." $5-10.

Advertising Postcard [on top]. Unused, real color photo, 6" x 4.25", by Airstream, unnumbered, c. 1990s. Caption: "Airstream Safari Travel Trailer." Notice that on the three postcards on this page, it was Airstream that included a portion of another company's vehicle in its advertising pictures—rather than the other way around. $10-15.

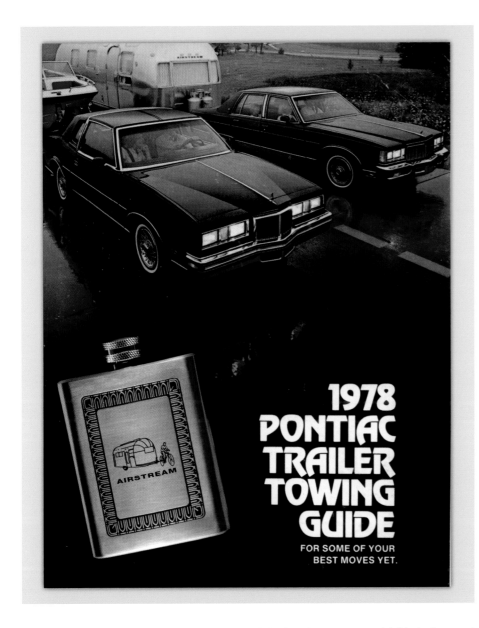

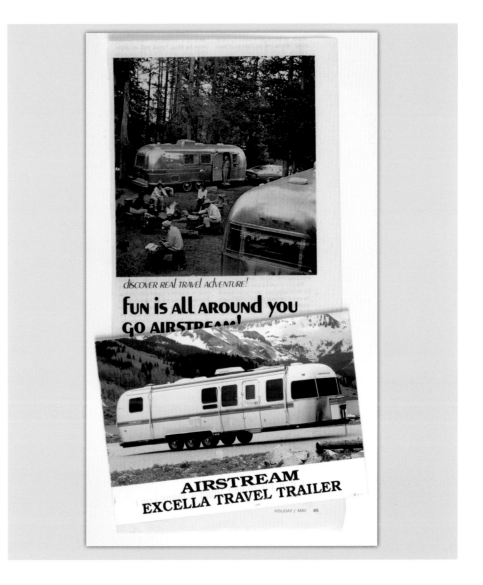

Advertising Brochure [underneath]. Light-weight brochure paper, tri-fold design, real color photo, 8.5" x 11" folded [25" x 11" unfolded], by General Motors, unnumbered, dated 1977. Title: *1978 Pontiac Trailer Towing Guide*. Airstream appeared again. $10-15.

Pocket Flask [on top]. Shiny silver metal, 3" x 4" x .75", by Zippo, #40086, c. 2000s. Imprint: "Airstream" with image of bicyclist pulling Airstream trailer. $30-40.

Magazine Advertisement [underneath]. Standard magazine paper, real color photo, 4.75" x 10.25", in *HOLIDAY*, c. 1970s. Caption: "Discover real travel adventure! ... Fun is all around you. ... Go Airstream." The text of this ad sent a favorite and apropos Airstream message: "When you own an Airstream travel trailer, all your dreams of travel adventure suddenly become practical reality!" $5-10.

Advertising Postcard [on top]. Used, real color photo, 6" x 4.25", by Airstream, unnumbered, posted 1998. Caption: "Airstream Excella Travel Trailer." The text on the reverse side of this card announced the "model year end close-out" for the 1998 coaches, and the " '99 model introduction" at Sun RV Superstore in Dade City, Florida, from October 15-25, 1998. This postcard was sent from Airstream headquarters in Jackson Center, Ohio, to a prospective buyer in Seminole, Florida. $10-15.

ARGOSY/MINUET FOR 1980

1980 ARGOSY
31 Rear Bath Model

1980 ARGOSY

When you hitch up to a 1980 **Argosy,** you'll be touring in a 25-, 28-, or 31-foot luxury machine–built with equal amounts of common sense and fashion sense. You'll have accommodations to sleep four, and the option to sleep seven, comfortably. As well as easy-to-care-for furnishings and ample storage for long-distance or short-term traveling.

1980 MINUET

If you're economy-minded, check out the new breed of Minuets in compact 20-, 22-, and 24-foot lengths. They're the lightest of all to tow. The most affordable, too. With room to sleep from four to seven-light, towable Minuets are for growing families who want to keep going. In style.

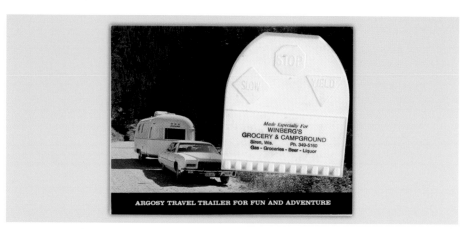

ARGOSY TRAVEL TRAILER FOR FUN AND ADVENTURE

Advertising Postcard [underneath]. Unused, real color photo, large 7" x 5.25", by Airstream, unnumbered, c. 1970s. Caption: "Argosy Travel Trailer For Fun And Adventure." Bravo! This hard-to-find ad card for Argosy looks exactly like numerous other outstanding Airstream postcards in size, colors, composition, and scenery. $30-40.

Novelty Snow Scraper [on top]. Hard plastic, black & off-white graphics, 3.5" x 4", no maker, unnumbered, c. 1960s. Inscription: "Made Especially for Weinberg's Grocery & Campground ... Siren, Wis. ..." When we first saw this piece, we immediately recognized its resemblance to the front or rear image of an Argosy trailer in both color and shape. On the reverse side is a clip mechanism to attach the ice scraper to a car's window visor, and its bottom section design is pointed/sharp plastic with wide plastic teeth to facilitate scraping snow and ice from vehicle windows. $20-25.

Advertising Brochure. Heavy paper, real color photo, 8.5" x 11", 2-page [front & back], by Airstream, unnumbered, dated 1980. Title: *Argosy/Minuet For 1980.* The Argosy/Minuet line by Airstream in the 1970s to about 1980 was a very stylish coach series, with the same streamline shape as its aluminum-bullet trailers, but with an exterior off-white or cream color paint finish. Airstream discontinued the Argosy/Minuet after about a decade in production, and later attempted a brief and unsuccessful revival of a boxy-shaped trailer with the Argosy name. $20-25.

Advertising Postcard. Unused, real color photo, 5.5" x 3.5", by dynacolor graphics, #P1614, c. 1970s. This card publicized the Jackson Travel Trailer Park in Jackson, Tennessee, and right in the center of the picture was a handsome Airstream Argosy trailer. If you look very closely, you can see two aluminum Airstream trailers parked to the right side of the photograph. $15-20.

Chapter 3

AIRSTREAM At Rest

Travel trailers and campgrounds go together. They are interrelated; they work together. Each depends upon the other. This chapter is about the Airstream at rest, namely, parked in a campsite somewhere around the country. We had hundreds of postcards and advertisements from which to select to compose this chapter, since we expect to see travel trailers at campgrounds, and Airstreams seem to be everywhere.

There have been thousands of advertising pictures of Airstreams situated in campgrounds, because both Airstream and RV park owners recognize the value of publicity photos showing the comfort, tranquility, convenience, and security of an Airstream trailer at rest at a campsite. The contrast of the Airstream's streamline design and aluminum shine against the backdrop of one of nature's camp settings is inviting and sometimes even captivating. Indeed, as campgrounds are shown that are more remote and primitive, the contrast between the rugged outdoors and the sleek Airstreams becomes even more dramatic and electrifying.

For folks who would like to spend a night or nights in an Airstream trailer, another opportunity to do so has been established—at a few KOA Kampgrounds. An article in the Summer 2009 issue of *AIRSTREAM LIFE* entitled "Finally You Can Rent An Airstream" by our friend Rich Luhr, the Editor of *AIRSTREAM LIFE*, describes the plan to have 25 Airstreams available for rent at KOA parks in Bar Harbor, Maine; Sugarloaf Key, Florida; and, Las Vegas, Nevada.

Advertising Postcard. Unused, multi-color linen, 5.5" x 3.5", by Curteich, #9B-H1695, c. 1940s. Caption: "Trailer Camp, Municipal Lakeside Park, Seneca Lake, Watkins Glen, N.Y. ... In the Finger Lakes Region." This card publicized a public campground. The local, state, and national governments recognized the many advantages to providing facilities for RVing. Notice the handsome Airstream parked under the trees on the right hand side of the picture, and on the far left side, there seems to have been a small rear side section of an Airstream. $15-20.

Magazine Advertisement [underneath]. Standard magazine paper, real black & white photo, 5" x 11", by Airstream, c. 1967. Caption: "Fun Is All Around You … Go Airstream!" What a great advertising strategy and photo, with some 90% of the picture showing the mountains and forest, and with only about 10% devoted to the Airstream trailer. This space allocation effectively brought home the point of the ad to "discover real travel adventure." Airstream's marketers were so masterful with language and imagery. For example, this ad said: "When just dreaming no longer satisfies that burning desire to travel, go Airstream and watch all your travel dreams come true!" $5-10.

Advertising Postcard [on top]. Used, real color photo, 5.5" x 3.5" by Camperama, unnumbered, posted 1979. Caption: "Camperama – Townsend, Vermont." Look at all of the elements in this classic campground promotional piece—a wilderness setting, an on-the-water campsite, an American flag (on the optional trailer flag pole), a canoe on the car's roof, a bright and sunny day, and an Airstream! Who could ask for more? The RVers who sent the postcard wrote in their message to friends in New York that they were staying three days at this RV park in southern Vermont. $10-15.

Advertising Brochure. Standard heavy brochure paper, multi-color graphic, 8.25" x 11", by Chevrolet, unnumbered, 12 pages, copyright 1972. Entitled: *1973 Chevrolet Trailering Guide.* The outdoor scene on the front of this brochure could almost have been painted by Norman Rockwell—it is so serene and appealing. The Airstream is a fitting prop in the picture, because the printed Chevy slogan at the front bottom recited: "Building a better way, to see the U.S.A." There is also another image of an Airstream with a Chevy station wagon tow vehicle on page 5 of this brochure. $20-25.

Advertising Postcard. Used, linen, 5.5" x 3.5", by Nationwide Post Card, unnumbered, c. 1950s [posted 1963]. Caption: "301 Trailer Park & Grocery … U.S. 301, 5 Miles North … Statesboro, Georgia." Often, these campground postcards were used for many years. Thus, although the RV park and the RVs visiting it may have changed, sometimes the postcards were not changed and updated. Note the emphasis on the presence of a grocery, an important convenience for campers, especially in earlier days, who could not carry much in the way of varieties or quantities of food staples. The campers who sent this card to family members in Maine had stayed the night in this park. An Airstream is centered in the photo, with a Spartan brand trailer to the right side. $20-25.

Tourist Postcard. Unused, real color photo, 5.5" x 4", by Elba Systems, #FS-2, dated 1968. What an unusual postcard. Here is a pleasant and restful Airstream scene, but there is no indication that the card is an advertisement for either Airstream or a particular campground. The back of the card bears no name or information other than that of its manufacturer and the year of production. $20-25.

RV Toy Model. Scarce Airstream replica toy, 8" x 2" x 2.5", by Design Studio of California, c. 1980s. This outstanding toy is a model of a 1956 coach, which would have been built in about the 25th year of Airstream's life. Notice the fine attention to details—including the unique thirteen-panel roof-ends design, the striped window curtains (done in the classic white and Airstream blue colors), the tandem axles with four tires, and the slimp or pivot wheel under the arm of the tow hitch. This spectacular Airstream toy is rarely available in the collectibles marketplace, especially with its original box [which we still have]. $200-250.

Advertising Postcard. Unused, real color photo, 3.5" x 5.5", no maker, #360421, c. 1970s. Caption: "Overnite Trailer Inn … East I-40 and Lakeside … Amarillo, Texas 79105." The text on the reverse side noted this campground was the "[n]ewest and finest park in Amarillo." There were two Airstreams parked in the foreground, and three flags flying [one of which was the Confederate flag, and that flag on the card adds value because some people collect postcards with such flags]. $20-25.

Advertising Postcard. Unused, real color photo, 6" x 4", by Max Friedl Photos, #166560, c. 1980s. This four-image card publicized a huge campground with 617 sites, called Tip-O-Texas RV Village in the Rio Grande Valley in Pharr, Texas. The park's many amenities included tennis courts, chapel, two swimming pools & spas, shuffleboard courts, pool room, and more. An Airstream was shown in the upper right quadrant. With so many campsites, there should have been many RVs from which to select for this photo opportunity. Yet, Airstream was chosen. $5-10.

Magazine Advertisement [above]. Standard magazine paper, black & white photo, small 5" x 4", by Airstream, c. 1970s. Caption: "Discover Real Travel Adventure!" In its ads, Airstream emphasized the comforts of its self-contained coaches, especially its larger trailers, by calling its models Land Yachts. As this piece promised: "Airstream Land Yachting means real travel independence." $5-10.

Advertising Postcard [below]. Used, real color photograph, 5.5" x 3.5", by Dexter Press & Greear Studio, unnumbered, posted 1975. What a lovely card—with the apple blossoms and the Airstream. This card publicizes the Wytheville KOA in Virginia, which is still in operation, having grown into an even prettier RV park over the years. The Airstream was center stage in the picture, even though the ad was for the campground. The message on the back of the card (from campers who were staying at this KOA) said something we have all written on a postcard at one time or another: "We will be home before you receive this card." $10-15.

Advertising Postcard. Unused, real color photo, 6" x 4", by Terrence Moore, unnumbered, c. 1990s. This publicity card promotes Shady Dell in Bisbee, Arizona. Yahoo! It's a unique traveler's experience, and one of our favorite places. At Shady Dell, visitors get the opportunity [if they book a reservation well in advance] to spend the night(s) in one of several restored vintage travel trailers, such as a Crown, El Rey, Spartan, or, of course, Airstream. There is also an original 1957 diner next door. We loved staying in the trailers and eating at the diner. Notice the Airstream in the center of the picture. $10-15.

Advertising Postcard. Used, real color photo, 5.5" x 3.5", by Dexter Press & LaMar Williams, #27165-B, c. 1950s-60s [posted 1961]. This well-known promotional card for National Trailer Park and Sales of Jackson Hole, Wyoming shows two Airstreams parked on the left hand side of the picture. $5-10.

Advertising Postcard. Unused, real color photo, 5.5" x 3.5", by Western Resort Publications & Ferris Scott, #542588 & #FS-780, c. late 1950s-early 1960s. Caption: "Greetings from Death Valley Texas Campground." Not surprisingly, the picture on this RV park postcard was taken in the winter season, when RVers flock to Death Valley, and there was an Airstream just left of center. $5-10.

Advertising Postcard. Used, real color photo, 5.5" x 3.5", by F.L. Davisson, #KV2020, posted 1970. This card publicized the Yuma Overnight Trailer Park of Yuma, Arizona, and there were two Airstreams on the right side of the photograph. You can tell this is a vintage card, because it listed a "refrigerated lounge" and "shuffleboard" as two of the campground amenities. $5-10.

Advertising Postcards. [Left] Unused, real color photo, 5.5" x 3.5", by Color-King, #49912, c. 1970s. Caption: "Little River Land Harbors of America." This card promoted the luxury RV resort Little Rivers Land Harbors on the famous Grand Strand along South Carolina's coast. Amenities included a swimming pool, tennis courts, and boat dock. The pictured Airstream, with its classy striped awning, is nestled on a shaded site with an expansive deck for outdoor living. $15-20.

[Right] Unused, real color photo, 5.5" x 3.5", by Color-King, #48851,52, c. 1970s. Caption: "Linville Land Harbor of America." Here is another card for the same high-end campground developer. This resort, located on a 1,000-acre tract "just off the Blue Ridge Parkway in Avery County, North Carolina," had amenities that included golf, tennis, sailing, fishing, and swimming. The Airstream trailer pictured on the postcard seems to fit right in at this upscale site. $15-20.

Advertising Postcard. Unused, real color photo, 5.5" x 3.5", by Don Studios, #P2738, c. 1970s. This campground card for Apple Valley Travel Park of Hendersonville, North Carolina, shows an Airstream parked in a picture-perfect setting, with a concrete patio, a picnic table with table cloth, shade trees, lawn chairs, potted flowers, and the classic striped Airstream awning. $20-25.

Advertising Postcard. Used, real color photo, 5.5" x 3.5", by Glacier Studio, unnumbered, posted 1970. This card advertised West Shore K.O.A. Kampground in Montana, near Glacier National Park, and on the back of the card, this KOA called itself: "The camper's home away from home." The Airstream actually seemed to appear more prominently in the picture than the A-frame KOA office building. Interestingly, this card was sent by Canadian RVers (who stayed at this KOA) to friends in Canada. Look at the next card and its description. $10-15.

Collector Wrist Watch [left]. Shiny stainless steel metal, 1.5" circular face, Airstream name & trailer image on face, unnumbered, c. 2000s. This watch, which keeps quite accurate time, has a simple and handsome face with a contemporary silver Airstream illustrated. $30-40.

RV Toy [right]. Shiny silver heavy metal, 3.75" x 1.25" x 1.5", reproduction of a 1949 Airstream Clipper, by Mattel - Hot Wheels [made in China], unnumbered, copyright 2000. This small-scale, quality toy model is a highly accurate reproduction, with two working/rolling wheels and a tow hitch, which allows it to be attached to a toy tow vehicle. It even showed the riveted construction of the trailer's exterior and the famous thirteen curved roof panels of the classic Airstream trailers. $30-40.

Advertising Postcard. Used, real color photo, 3.5" x 5.5", by Reny Brothers Printers, #31799, posted 1966. This publicity card is a bit unusual, although as the preceding card tends to show, a lot of Canadian RVers visit the U.S. This postcard advertised Wild Acres Tent & Trailer Park in Old Orchard Beach, Maine. But, ink-stamped on the back of the card is this inscription: "State of Maine Publicity Bureau, 900 Dorchester Street West, Queen Elizabeth Hotel, Montreal, Quebec" [Canada]. And, the card was sent from Montreal with a Canadian postage stamp to another city in Quebec. Curious circumstances ... if the state government was promoting a private campground to potential visitors from another country. Nevertheless, again an Airstream appeared front and center on this card. $10-15.

Advertising Postcard. Used [but not mailed], real color photo, 5.5" x 3.5", by G.R. Brown Company, #J9710, dated 1984 [handwritten note on back]. The Airstream pictured here was parked at the Grand Marias Recreation Area in Grand Marias, Minnesota, and this recreation area is open year round—even throughout the harsh Minnesota winter. Many people will buy a postcard and keep it as a souvenir of their travels, rather than mail it to someone else. Often a note is written on the back of the card to record the date of the trip, as was the case here. $5-10.

Advertising Postcard. Unused, real color photo, 5.5" x 3.5", by Western Resort Publications & Ferris Scott, #S-15799-1 & #FS-92, c. 1970s. Caption: "Fawnskin ... Big Bear Lake." Both this card and the adjacent postcard showed Fawnskin Camp Grounds in Big Bear Lake, California, and the text on the back of both cards was identical. But, the pictures on the two cards were different, except that both included Airstream trailers parked toward the left side of the photos. $10-15.

Advertising Postcard. Used [but not mailed], real color photo, 5.5" x 3.5", by Curteichcolor & Robert Hecht Enterprises, #3DK-939, dated 1966 [handwritten note on back]. Yahoo! Three Airstreams were parked in the same row of trailers. This picturesque and patriotic card advertised B & B Trailer Village in Jackson, Wyoming. The note on the back said: "We stayed here Aug. 10-11, 1966." $10-15.

Advertising Postcard. Unused, real color photo, 5.5" x 3.5", by Western Resort Publications, #FS-1337 & #S102186L3, c. 1970s. Caption: "Fawnskin ... Big Bear Lake." This ad card publicized Fawnskin Camp Grounds in Big Bear Lake, California. The back of the card announced that "trailer folk make this their headquarters ... one of the most popular camping spots in Southern California." Look closely and you will notice that this card was actually a split-image picture of two similar scenes. An Airstream rested at the far left bottom of the left-hand picture. $10-15.

Advertising Postcard. Unused, real color photo, 3.5" x 5.5", by McGrew Color Graphics & Aerex High Bridge, #141508, c. 1970s. Caption: "Bucktail Camping Resort." This split-image card advertised Bucktail Camping Resort in the mountains near Mansfield, Pennsylvania. A long Airstream was parked in the upper right hand corner of the top picture. $10-15.

Magazine Advertisement [left]. Standard magazine paper, real color photo, 5" x 10", by Airstream, dated 1971. Caption: "Fulfill Your Dreams of a Happy Retirement … Go Airstream … The Better Way To Travel!" The writers for Airstream advertising wrote very effectively. For example, in this ad: "Remember the promise you made to yourself when the children were growing up? … that you would some day take time out to 'live a little.' Now it's your turn to live! Travel far and travel wide … discover a whole world of new friends and interests. … Do it soon … you've got a lot of living to do!" And look at the accompanying image—a night scene, with a western desert backdrop, a roaring campfire, a horse and rider, and, of course, an Airstream. $5-10.

Advertising Postcard [right]. Unused, real color photo, 4" x 9", by McCoy, #15923, c. 1970s. Caption: "St. Augustine Beach [Florida] KOA Kampground." This large-scale, rectangular, multi-view type card was popular in earlier years, though not so much now. It was big enough to include a sizable map to be printed on the back to provide directions to the campground. And, in the middle of the images on the card's front appeared an Airstream nestled in a shaded campsite. $15-20.

Advertising Brochure [underneath]. Standard brochure paper, real color photos, 8.25" x 11", by General Motors, #89-88USA, 22 pages, c. 1988-89. Entitled: *GMC Truck Trailering*. The pleasant waterfront camping scene on the front of this booklet showed only a portion of the exterior front section of an Airstream at the far right hand edge of the picture, but the fact that the trailer was an Airstream was unmistakable. There are two other pictures of Airstreams in tow by GMC trucks on inside pages 12-13 of the brochure. $10-15.

Advertising Postcard [on top]. Used [but not mailed], real color photo, 5.5" x 3.5", by Tichnor Brothers, #K-17524, dated 1972 [handwritten note on back]. This card publicized a primitive-style trailer park, which had neither electric nor water connections, called Gulpha Gorge Campground near Hot Springs Mountain and the city of Hot Springs, Arkansas. As so often happens, an Airstream was the sole RV shown and was centered in the picture. Airstream advertisements frequently emphasized the self-contained nature of Airstreams, so that there was no need for hookups to water and electricity. As the adjacent magazine ad noted: "An Airstream travel trailer offers you the ultimate in travel/living luxury … totally independent of outside sources." $10-15.

Advertising Postcard. Unused, real color photo, 5.5" x 3.5", by Dexter Press & Connelly Press, #66345-B, c. 1970s. This card showed Lakeside Trailer Park, an adults only campground, on Lake Hamilton in Hot Springs National Park, Arkansas. And sure enough, there was an Airstream parked right on a lakefront site near the left hand side of the picture. $10-15.

Advertising Postcard. Unused, real color photo, 5.5" x 3.5", by Dukane Press & Marsh Post Card Service, #1630, c. 1960s. Caption: "Greetings From Cherokee Campground, Jekyll Island, Georgia." The stylish Cadillac and handsome Airstream looked quite good sitting next to one another in the center of this picture. $10-15.

Advertising Postcard. Unused, real color photo, 3.5" x 5.5", by Aladdin Color, #133718, copyright 1973. This split-image card advertised Seashore Campsites in Cape May, New Jersey. Sometimes, when we read the descriptions of campgrounds on advertising cards dating back 30-40 years ago, certain features seem unusual by today's standards. For instance, among the numerous amenities at this park, the card listed an "ice house … coin-operated hot showers … flushing toilets … drinking water … laundry tubs." Today, these features might conjure up images of Ma & Pa Kettle camping there. What is the only brand of RV pictured at this park? Airstream. $15-20.

Advertising Postcard. Unused, real color photo, 5.5" x 3.5", by Dexter Press & Photography by Norton, #98580-C, c. 1970s. Amazing … four Airstreams at rest in one campground! Three Airstreams were parked on the left side of the picture, and one was on the right. This card promoted Trailerland Park in Anaheim, California, which was right across the road from Disneyland. $10-15.

Advertising Postcard. Unused, real color photo, 5.5" x 3.5", by T.N. Gilbert & Associates, #113477, c. 1970s. Wow! It's a "hat trick." Three Airstreams appeared on this card, which promoted Fiesta Key Resort in Fiesta Key, Florida. As the back of the card promised [presumably for RVers in the winter months]: "Fiesta Key Is The Place To Be." $10-15.

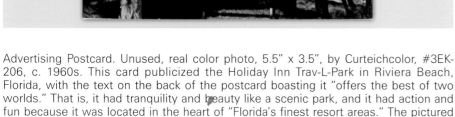

Advertising Postcard. Unused, real color photo, 5.5" x 3.5", by Curteichcolor, #3EK-206, c. 1960s. This card publicized the Holiday Inn Trav-L-Park in Riviera Beach, Florida, with the text on the back of the postcard boasting it "offers the best of two worlds." That is, it had tranquility and beauty like a scenic park, and it had action and fun because it was located in the heart of "Florida's finest resort areas." The pictured Airstream seemed quite comfortably at rest in this upscale campground. $15-20.

Advertising Postcard. Used, real black & white photos, 6-image, 5.5" x 3.5", no maker, unnumbered, posted 1961. Caption: "Val Verde Motel and Trailer Courts ... Highway 83 ... Donna, Texas." This rare, six-image postcard was sent in January from Alamo, Texas, to Fort Atkinson, Wisconsin, with the handwritten message on the card's back announcing that the senders would be staying at this campsite for a month. Notice the Airstream parked in the top middle picture. $20-25.

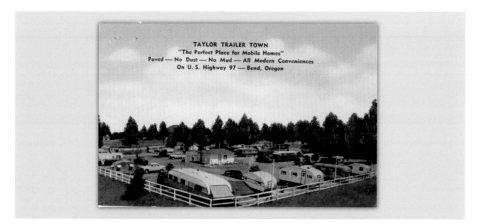

Advertising Postcard. Unused, multi-color linen, 5.5" x 3.5", by E. C. Kropp, #26944N, c. 1950s. Caption: "Taylor Trailer Town ... 'The Perfect Place For Mobile Homes' ... Paved – No Dust – No Mud – All Modern Conveniences ... On U.S. Highway 97 – Bend, Oregon." This interesting and scarce card also stated in the text on its reverse side that the trailer park had "immaculately clean rest rooms" and that it was "quiet – off the road – no trains." In the picture on the far right of the postcard was an Airstream, but instead of it being a shiny silver-aluminum color, it ended up appearing as a green trailer when the color was applied to the card. $20-25.

Desk Set. Thick leather & gold-plate stainless steel, scissors, letter opener, & sheath, 10" x 3.25", by Airstream, unnumbered, c. 1960s-70s. This piece is highly unusual, as we have never seen another like it. It appears to have been done by Airstream or at least authorized by Airstream, because the name "Airstream" was printed in bold letters down the length of the leather sheath with a small silver-colored metal Airstream trailer [1.5" x .5"] also affixed. The scissors were marked as made in Italy. This set would look handsome and fitting resting on any home or office desk—so, we included it here in the chapter called "Airstream At Rest." $50-75.

AIRSTREAM Aerials

The shiny and aerodynamic Airstream trailer does not simply look good from ground level. Its striking and unique image is also impressive and unmistakable from above. Not surprisingly, the folks at Airstream recognized this fact early, and Airstream and other advertisers have taken repeated steps to capitalize on it. Thus, countless photographs taken from on high have captured the rooftops of Airstreams in a wide variety of settings.

We have never seen any RV manufacturer, other than Airstream, use an aerial picture in its own advertising for its coaches—as other RV roofs simply do not look very good. Those other rooftops are neither streamlined nor stylish. Indeed, other travel trailer tops are almost always flat (which is not the best design for rain or snow), and those other RV roofs are littered with air-conditioners, exhaust and plumbing vents, satellite dishes, and various antennas (which does not add style to an already plain design). But, Airstream's sleek, rounded, and shiny rooftop is in a league all by itself.

The truth is that the single most popular viewpoint for campground advertising photos is the aerial picture. And, in an incredibly high proportion of all of the campsite aerial photos that we have reviewed [and we have looked at thousands of them], one or more Airstream trailers appears parked in the subject campgrounds. The fact that one or more Airstreams seems almost always to be present should not surprise anyone. After all, a lot of Airstreams have been produced, since Airstream has been in business longer than any other RV maker. Additionally, Airstream has been so well built and is so dependable that most of the Airstreams ever produced are still roadworthy and in use. Hence, you find them just about everywhere.

AIRSTREAM LAND YACHTING—THE BETTER WAY TO TRAVEL

Advertising Postcard. Unused, real color aerial photo, large 7" x 5.25", by Airstream, unnumbered, c. 1960s. Caption: "Airstream Land Yachting—The Better Way To Travel." This remarkable aerial image made such a favorable impression for Airstream, although the Airstream trailer occupied much less than 10% of the picture! Airstream has achieved incredible advantage from its idea to call its coaches "Land Yachts." Is there any other RV in the world that looks as good from above as an Airstream? Absolutely not. $20-25.

Advertising Brochure. Heavy paper, numerous real color photos, 8.25" x 11", by Airstream, unnumbered, 34 pages, dated 1978. Title: *The Airstream Story*. This handsome aerial picture appeared as the cover photo for the 1978 brochure, and similar brochures were published annually for many years as *The Airstream Story* to introduce each successive year's new models of Airstreams. These brochures told the history of Airstream in considerable detail, including many vintage pictures, and these booklets are highly sought by Airstream enthusiasts and collectors. Notice, again, how the image of the Airstream trailer was such a very small part of this photo. $50-75.

Advertising Postcard. Unused, real color aerial photo, 3.5" x 5.5", by Vic's Photos & Navajo Trail, #110174, c. 1970s. This aerial card pictured Moore & Moore Trailer Park in Cortez, California, revealing a long and narrow RV park with four Airstream trailers situated in its sites. Notice the symbols printed in the upper right hand corner of the photo to help in finding the park—both the North-South-East-West directions and the identification of route US 160. We have two cards for this park with the identical pictures on the front, but with slight differences in the text on the back of the cards [one card added the zip code to the address, and changed the names of the proprietors]. $10-15.

Advertising Postcard. Unused, real color aerial photo, 3.5" x 5.5", by Nationwide Golf & Printing, unnumbered, c. 1970s. Anyone traveling I-95 along the southern East Coast will have seen the many highway billboards promoting "South of the Border," which is a large multi-purpose commercial venture with tourist shops, restaurants, carnival rides, and an RV park called Pedro's Super Campground. This handsome, well-known aerial postcard advertised that campground, and an Airstream was captured in the center of its picture. $10-15.

Advertising Postcard. Unused, real color aerial photo, 5.5" x 3.5", by Dexter Press & Universal Studio, #72881-B, c. 1960s. This card publicizing ABC Trailer Sales of Leesburg, Florida, showed a group of fourteen Airstreams parked around its sales lot. Notice how distinctly different the Airstreams appear from the other trailers at this location—and this picture was taken from way up in the air! $15-20.

Advertising Postcard. Used [but not mailed], real color aerial photo, 5.5" x 3.5", by California Color Photos & Dexter Press, #480-D, dated 1976 [handwritten note on back]. This card promoted Holiday Harbor trailer park on Shasta Lake near the McCloud River in California. Two long Airstreams stand out from all the other RVs in the picture—and, they always will. $10-15.

Advertising Postcard. Used, real color aerial photo, 5.5" x 3.5", by Smith Aerial Surveys & Dukane Press, #8234, posted 1969. Caption: "Boating, Fishing, Swimming … Direct access to the ocean." The Yacht Haven Mobile Home Park in Fort Lauderdale, Florida, was shown from above on this card. The senders' handwritten message on the back said, "This is living. We are very happy with this location." The postcard was sent from Fort Lauderdale to East Hampton, New York. How appropriate that this park was named "Yacht Haven," because there was an Airstream Land Yacht situated amongst all the large mobile homes [to the right side of the short canal shown in the lower right quadrant of the picture]. $10-15.

Magazine Advertisement [above]. Standard magazine paper, real black & white aerial photo, 5.5" x 4.25", by Airstream, c. 1960s. Caption: "Discover Real Travel Adventure." The inviting beach scene on this ad seemed to fit the caption perfectly. And further, as the effective text of the ad suggested: "You just tow your Airstream lightly behind your car and follow your travel whims wherever they urge you to go." $5-10.

Advertising Postcard [below]. Unused, real color aerial photo, large 7" x 5.25", by Airstream, unnumbered, c. 1960s. Caption: "Airstream Land Yachting—The Better Way To Travel." The spectacular aerial photo of an Airstream on the beach on this actual postcard was the same picture as the black and white image on the magazine ad above, and this strategy was as it should be. Why should Airstream use a fantastic photo only once? $25-50.

Advertising Postcard. Unused, real color aerial photo, 5.5" x 3.5", by Steen Enterprises, #641094, c. 1970s. Caption: "Kaiser's KOA, Coburg, Oregon." This aerial photo was taken from a considerable distance above the KOA campground, but two Airstream trailers are clearly visible [and there are only about 17 RVs in the park]. The picture was undoubtedly taken from a height and an angle that allowed the photographer to include Interstate 5 in the scene [along the top of the card], to show ready access to the campground, and vice versa. However, the 2011-2012 KOA Directory does not list a KOA campground in the Coburg-Eugene vicinity. $10-15.

Advertising Postcard. Unused, real color aerial photo, 5.5" x 3.5", by Max Friedl Photo, #R28130, c. 1980s. Unbelievable! Nine Airstreams! This impressive aerial card promoted Emerald Grove Travel Park in Harlingen, Texas, announcing in the text on the back of the postcard that Emerald Grove was "[a] beautiful place to spend your winter." And, it was certainly even more beautiful with so many Airstreams parked there. Perhaps, an Airstream caravan or rally was in progress. $10-15.

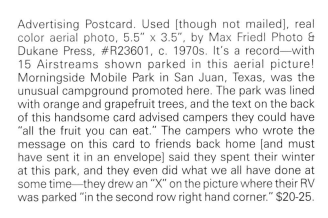

Advertising Postcard. Used [though not mailed], real color aerial photo, 5.5" x 3.5", by Max Friedl Photo & Dukane Press, #R23601, c. 1970s. It's a record—with 15 Airstreams shown parked in this aerial picture! Morningside Mobile Park in San Juan, Texas, was the unusual campground promoted here. The park was lined with orange and grapefruit trees, and the text on the back of this handsome card advised campers they could have "all the fruit you can eat." The campers who wrote the message on this card to friends back home [and must have sent it in an envelope] said they spent their winter at this park, and they even did what we all have done at some time—they drew an "X" on the picture where their RV was parked "in the second row right hand corner." $20-25.

Old Aluminum Adventures

Wally Byam's 1956 European Caravan

One Family's Experience

By Fred Coldwell

Norma Miller's 48-page article "Through Europe by Trailer Caravan," describing her family's participation in Wally Byam's 1956 European Caravan, appears in the June, 1957 issue of National Geographic magazine. Illustrated by her husband's stunning color photography, it is the most thorough mid-century description of caravanning in Airstream trailers, and belongs in the library of every Airstream enthusiast. We recently interviewed Norma for a behind the scenes look at that caravan and how it introduced her and her family to a lifetime of Airstream adventures.

In summer 1955, before they owned a travel trailer, the Miller family – father Ardean, an established commercial photographer, Norma, and the boys, Randy 9 and twins Brad and Bruce, 7-1/2 – headed west in their car from Florida to see America. The trip was unpleasant. Nightly motel accommodations had to be found every evening and luggage had to be shuttled in and out. Everyone slept in different beds of varying quality and cleanliness each night, and the rooms often reeked of stale smoke. Restaurant dining was expensive and was limited to items on the menu. The boys would have been perfectly content with peanut butter and jelly sandwiches or soup for breakfast, but such food was not available in motel

28 AIRSTREAM LIFE FALL 2007

FALL 2007 AIRSTREAM LIFE 29

Magazine Article. Standard magazine paper, real color photos, 8" x 11", "Wally Byam's 1956 European Caravan: One Family's Experience," by Fred Coldwell, in *AIRSTREAM LIFE*, Fall 2007, pages 28-35. This interesting and informative article included several Ardean Miller pictures, and the piece began with this creative and memorable, large aerial photo (which occupies almost two pages of the magazine) of some of the now-retro tow cars and their Airstream partners in Dusseldorf, Germany, where a brass band had greeted the caravanners. Since at least the 1950s, the people at Airstream (and at many other advertisers) have understood that Airstream is uniquely recognizable and attractive not only from the ground level, but also from above. For the article, $5-10.

Advertising Postcard. Unused, real color aerial photo, 5.5" x 3.5", by C. Hettesheimer, #120,182, c. 1980s. Handsome RV postcard! This aerial publicity card for Ralph's Trailer Park in Zephyrhills, Florida, pictured at least four Airstream trailers among the many RVs parked there. $10-15.

Advertising Postcard. Used, real color aerial photo, 5.5" x 3.5", by Wasman Photography, #150416, posted 1977. This card publicized the Recreational Vehicle Park of Eustis, Florida, by way of an aerial picture that showed at least seven Airstream trailers. Some of those Airstreams can be identified by seeing only a very small fraction of their rooftops, but it only takes a glance at a tiny portion to know it's an Airstream. The postcard was sent from Florida to Butler, Pennsylvania. $10-15.

Advertising Postcard. Unused, real color aerial photo, 5.5" x 3.5". by Carl Schultz, #S30744, c. 1960s. Caption: "Bella-Vista Mobile Homes Lodge" [in Cayucos, California]. Even though the name suggested this park was a mobile home lodge, the text on the back of the card said it was available for "overnight stops," and the photo showed several travel trailers at rest in this park. This promotional postcard included the roof of an Airstream in the center of the picture. $10-15.

RV Trailer Toy. Heavy metal with rubber tires, silver & black graphics, 5.25" x 2" x 2.25", replica of 1953 Airstream, by Brooklin Models [England], #54, c. 1990s. Brooklin is one of England's premiere toy manufacturers, comparable to the Franklin Mint in the USA in regard to its production of weighty and highly-detailed upscale toy models [intended for adult collectors, and not intended for child's play]. Curiously, the bottom of the toy was marked "1953 American Caravan" [the term many Europeans use for an RV], while the name "Airstream" was faithfully printed on both the front and rear of the coach just as it would have appeared on an actual trailer. The attention to detail was remarkable—including seven curved front and rear roof panels, the famous Airstream door-in-door design of the side entry door, the riveted construction of the exterior, the roof features [stove pipe and vents], the propane bottles, and so forth. This coach even had whitewall tires and a vanity license plate "BRK 54" (meaning Brooklin 1954). Superb quality! $75-100.

Advertising Postcard. Unused, real color aerial photo, large 7" x 5.25", by Airstream, unnumbered, c. 1970s. Caption: "Airstream Land Yachting—The Better Way To Travel." We are constantly amazed at how effective Ardean Miller's photography for Airstream could have been when, as he did in this instance, he tucked the Airstream trailer away in the bottom left corner of the picture. But, it was inspired! $30-40.

RV Light Set. Cardboard box packaging & plastic light set, multi-color graphic, 11" x 8.5", by Sue Scott & Primal Lite, unnumbered, copyright 1992. Entitled: "Ramblin' Road Light Set." Too cute! This fun scene appeared on the top cover of the RV light set, and the graphic was complete with lizards on the road, cows in the field, and painted-desert type hill formations on the horizon. The detailed graphic also showed an aerial view of a vintage RV pair—a small Rambler-style tow car and a short Airstream-style travel trailer—venturing down a narrow two-lane western roadway. Curiously, the plastic trailer in the cardboard box had an Airstream-blue color, while the trailer on the box itself was silver in color—like an Airstream. And, both versions of the coaches have riveted, panel construction—like a real Airstream. For the set, $30-40.

Advertising Postcard. Unused, real color aerial photo, 5.5" x 4.25", by Vistaprint, unnumbered, c. 2000s. Caption: "Moose River Campground ... Saint Johnsbury, Vermont." This picturesque, quiet, adult RV park is one of our favorites in the country [see mooserivercampground.com]. Its owners and operators, Mary and Gary, have become good friends of ours over the course of our numerous visits, and they seem just about always to have one or more Airstreams in residence—as was the case when the picture for this card was taken. With a magnifying glass, you can see an Airstream parked in a shaded river-side site in the middle area toward the left side of the postcard. $10-15.

Advertising Postcard. Unused, real color aerial photo, 5.5" x 3.5", by Shed Enterprises & Dukane Press, #8602, c. 1970s. This card advertised the Chateau Chaparral in Nathrop, Colorado, and the postcard and the campground were doubly unique. First, according to the text on the back of the card, the concept of this RV park was to provide "new, exciting, dude ranch facilities for campers," such as "good fishing in our mountain streams, trail rides, [and] chuck wagon meals." Second, at the time when this aerial picture was taken there must have been an Airstream rally going on, or an Airstream caravan passing through, because a very close look at the photo shows twenty Airstream trailers parked here. Yahoo! $20-25.

Advertising Postcard. Unused, multi-color chrome, 5.5" x 3.5", by Tichnor Brothers & A. S. Landis, #G89434, c. 1950s. Caption: "Riverside Trailer Park." This brightly colored aerial graphic of the Riverside Trailer Park in Holly Hill, Florida (near Daytona Beach), includes at least three Airstream trailers, with one appearing in the far left row of campsites and two shown in the center row. The description on the back of this wonderfully creative card suggests its vintage age, for it refers to such amenities as "bingo, canasta, shuffle board, individual trailer sewerage, and a filling station" and to the "Board of Health Inspection: Excellent." $20-25.

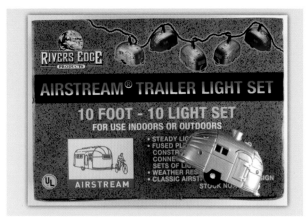

RV Light Set. Standard thin cardboard box packaging & plastic lights, multi-color graphics, 10.5" x 7.5", by Airstream & Rivers Edge Products, #419, copyright 2004. Title: "Airstream Trailer Light Set." Since this chapter is about "Airstream Aerials," we thought these Airstream RV lights should be included, because these lights usually hang in the air on the sides of RVs or on RV awnings. And, the individual plastic lights are quite good replicas of Airstream trailers. $20-25.

Advertising Postcard. Unused, real color aerial photo, 5.5" x 3.5", by George Skadding Photo & Dukane Press, #R25573, c. 1960s. Wow! At least eight Airstreams were shown here. Could this occasion have been an Airstream caravan or rally? The card promoted Highland Woods Travel Trailer Park in Pompano, Florida. $10-15.

Business Card. Standard business card stock, real color aerial photo, 3.5" x 2.25", c. 1970s. This aerial photo made a handsome front for a business card. We counted about twenty-two tiny Airstreams in the picture. The business named on the back of the card was Farnsworth Camping Center in Elysburg, Pennsylvania, which the text identified as a "Factory Authorized Airstream Dealer." $5-10.

AIRSTREAM LAND YACHTING—THE BETTER WAY TO TRAVEL

Advertising Postcard. Unused, real color aerial photo, 5.5" x 3.5", by J. C. Spencer, #83,972, c. 1970s. It seems that quite a number of KOA campground postcards included one or more Airstreams at rest in their parks. This aerial-image card advertised Astro KOA Kampground in Houston, Texas, and it showed at least three Airstreams parked there. This park is not listed in the 2011-2012 KOA Directory. Incidentally, KOA celebrates its 50th anniversary in 2012. $10-15.

Advertising Postcard. Unused, real color aerial photo, large 7" x 5.25", by Airstream, unnumbered, c. 1970. Caption: "Airstream Land Yachting—The Better Way To Travel." Time and time again, Airstream has so successfully used photographic images in which Airstream trailers occupy only a very small percentage of the total pictures—and in this case, it was an aerial view of only a small part of the trailer surrounded by the forest and the lake. $25-50.

Tourist Postcard. Used, real color aerial photo, 5.5" x 3.5", by H. S. Crocker & Golden West Color Card, unnumbered, posted 1966. The printed text on the back of this very popular card promoted "trailering along a fine stretch" of U.S. Highway 101 between Newport Harbor and Laguna Beach in Southern California. If you look closely, you will see that in the picture there was both an Airstream and an Airstream look-a-like, with both shown only by small pieces of those trailers. $10-15.

Magazine Article. Standard magazine paper, real black & white photos & color photos, 8" x 11", in *SMITHSONIAN*, "To Airstreamers, A Nomad's Life Is The Good Life," by Doug Stewart, December 1985, pages 74-83. The large aerial picture appearing early in this article showed an Airstream rally in Lake Placid, New York, in the summer of 1985 attended by over 3900 travel trailers. For the full issue, $15-20.

Magazine Advertisement [underneath]. Standard magazine paper, real black & white aerial photo, 7.5" x 11", by Sun-Free Awning, in *TRAILER LIFE*, May 1980. Caption: "Now every RV owner can afford a quality, automatic roll-up awning. … The Sun-Free Awning." Remarkable staging! Isn't it amazing this awning company wanted an Airstream in the advertising picture for its product so badly that it settled for such a tiny piece of an Airstream. This photograph showed an aerial shot of a very, very small part of the top of the roof of a vintage Airstream—next to the awning and trailer actually featured in the advertisement. $5-10.

Advertising Postcard. Unused, real color aerial photo, 4" x 6", by John Hopf, #52467, c. 1970s-80s. This unusual and scarce card advertised Meadowlark Mobile Home & Trailer Park in Middletown, Rhode Island. Interestingly, the printed text on the reverse side of the postcard pointed out that the campground was close to "mansions." Could that reference have meant Airstream Land Yachts? After all, if you look closely at the picture, you can count ten Airstreams in attendance. $15-20.

Advertising Postcard. Unused, real color aerial photo, 5.5" x 3.5", by Peterborough Post Card Company [Canada] & H. Oakman, #70577-B, c. 1970s. This card promoted the Miners Bay Lodge Trailer Park in Miners Bay, Ontario, Canada, in the Haliburton Highlands region. Though somewhat difficult to see without magnification, four Airstreams were parked along the beach near the bottom of the postcard. $10-15.

Advertising postcard [on top]. Unused, real color aerial photo, 5.5" x 3.5", by Stan Sheets Photography & Dexter Press, #22463-C, c. 1960s-70s. This card promoted The Anchorage Mobile Homes Park in Delray Beach, Florida, which must have been a strict place. According to the text on the reverse side, the park was for adults only, and no pets were allowed. Parked on the entrance street to this park in the bottom left corner of the picture was an Airstream and its tow car [perhaps waiting to see if its owners were going to be allowed in]. $10-15.

Chapter 5

AIRSTREAM Pieces

Because Airstream trailers are identifiable from every angle, often only fragments of Airstreams need to be shown in pictures. Whether the image displays the front or rear, one side or the other, or the top of an Airstream, it only takes a glimpse of a small area for an advertiser or photographer to take full advantage of the presence of an Airstream in a picture. In other words, part of an Airstream is better than none at all.

In fact, the most memorable of all the various Airstream angles has to be the rear view, for the back end of an Airstream sports its unique, shiny, rounded, and sectioned roof panels. Many Airstream bullet-shapes have been constructed with the classic thirteen-panel design, its traditional set of production serial numbers, and the Airstream name printed in black lettering. Even the contemporary models still have their panels of aluminum that are reminiscent of early airplane fuselages, as well as the standard black capital letters of the Airstream name. Importantly, countless Americans had their very first encounters with the rear-ends of Airstreams when they drove up behind them on the highways somewhere. And, it took only one sighting to cement a lifelong memory of the Airstream, regardless of the angle that was first observed.

As you look at the pieces shown and described in this chapter, look for the photo that shows the tiniest bit of an Airstream. And, notice how short a span of time it takes you to be sure it's an Airstream in that photo. You'll be amazed.

Quite arguably, this chapter constitutes the one that is most complimentary of Airstreams. What other authors of a book of images and photographs would dare to display only fragments of the objects that are the subject of their book?

Advertising Postcard. Used, real color photo, 5.5" x 3.5", by Robert Blondell & Dexter Press, unnumbered, posted 1981. Bits and pieces of three different Airstream trailers can be seen in the picture on this well-known card, which promoted Bay Pines Annex Travel Trailer Park in Seminole, Florida. The four ladies posed in the photo looked content, didn't they? Interestingly, the text on the back of the postcard noted, since many RVers are older folks, that the park was close to the Veterans' Hospital and to doctors' offices. The card was sent to Swisher, Iowa. $5-10.

Advertising Postcard. Used, real color photo, 5.5" x 3.5", by dynacolor graphics, #P24718, posted 1987. Caption: "Fort Tatham Campground ... Sylva, NC." What a coincidence! The text on the reverse side of the card emphasized that when staying at Fort Tatham you can "camp by a stream." And, as promised, the picture showed an Airstream at the campground. The senders of this card wrote in their message on the back that they had stayed at this RV park, and they sent their card from North Carolina to Oneonta, New York. Could the photographer have shown any smaller portion of the Airstream, and still have made it recognizable as an Airstream? Yes, as we will see a number of times in the remainder of this chapter. $15-20.

Advertising Brochure. Standard brochure paper, real black & white photos & graphics, 8.5" x 11", by Chrysler Motors, #81-270-1356, 8 pages, dated 1972. Title: '72 Dodge Trailer-Towing Requirements. What a hot, hot, hot pink background! Admittedly, the very small piece of the Airstream shown in the picture on the cover of this scarce booklet was made particularly easy to identify, since the "Airstream" name was printed on the front of the trailer. But, even without that helpful logo, the trailer would be readily recognizable. This brochure actually included two other photographs of Airstreams being pulled by Dodges, on pages 2 & 5. $20-25.

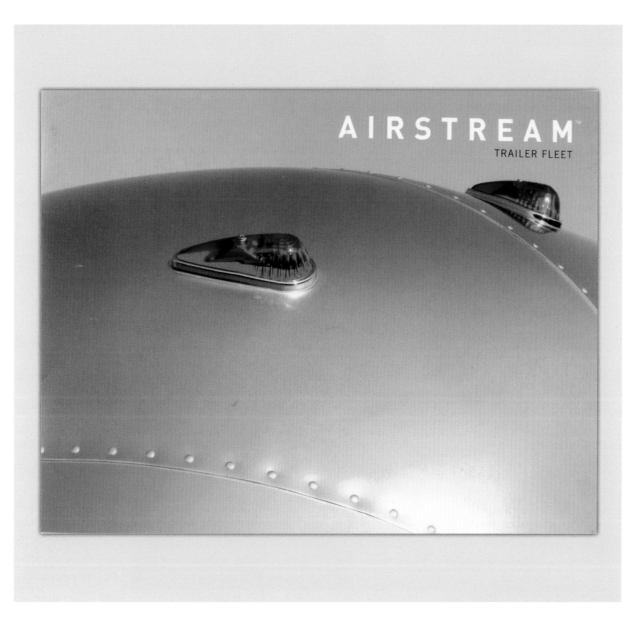

Advertising Brochure. Standard brochure cover and paper, real color photos, 11" x 8.5", by Airstream, unnumbered, 32 pages, c. 2000s. Title: *Airstream Trailer Fleet*. What a fantastic image of a piece of the roof of an Airstream on the cover of this brochure to prove the point of this chapter [cleverly called "Airstream Pieces"]. Airstream is so unique that a view of just a tiny morsel of its exterior will readily reveal its identity. For the brochure, $30-40.

Magazine Advertisement [underneath]. Standard magazine paper, real color photo, 5" x 11", by Airstream, dated 1971. Caption: "Fulfill your dreams of travel adventure—Go Airstream … The better way to travel!" In this picture, it was the front end of an Airstream that immediately identified it, but in the adjacent postcard it was the back end of an Airstream that had the same effect. $5-10.

Advertising Postcard [on top]. Used, real color photo, 5.5" x 3.5", by Clarendon Printing, #94,896, posted 1972. Caption [on the sign]: "Fairway Trailer Park" [in Manning, South Carolina]. On the reverse side, this card contained a sizable map with directions to the campground that took up half the space ordinarily available for senders' messages. Nevertheless, in perfect tiny handwriting, the senders wrote to friends in Maine that they had stayed at this RV park on their way to Florida (the card was mailed in April, which seems a little late to be headed to Florida). The rear portion of an Airstream was visible just left of center in the picture. $10-15.

Organization Postcard. Used, real black & white photo, 6" x 4", by Vintage Airstream Club, unnumbered, posted 2010. Caption: "We're missing you. Time to renew! The VAC sticker! Wear it like a badge of honor. VINTAGEAIRSTREAMCLUB.COM." How apropos in this chapter about "Airstream Pieces" to find that the Vintage Airstream Club has adopted just the classic eyes [windows] on the front of an early Airstream as a recognizable symbol. This chapter proves again and again that, with both vintage and newer Airstreams, a small segment from any number of locations on the coaches could identify them as Airstreams. $15-20.

Advertising Postcard. Used, real color photo, 5.5" x 3.5", by W. M. Cline Company & Color-King, #101142, posted 1969. This two-image card publicized Dudley Creek Travel Trailer Park in the Smokey Mountains in Gatlinburg, Tennessee. The printed text on the reverse side said this campground was "ideally located to park your 'home-away-from-home'." The partial image of an Airstream appeared in the far right bottom corner of the picture. A mom and dad who were staying at this RV park sent the postcard from Gatlinburg to their children in Columbus, Ohio. $5-10.

Fabric Patches. Tight-weaved fabric, multi-color graphics, 3" diameter circles, by Airstream & Airstream-affiliated groups, c. 1990s-2000s. Inscriptions: [left] "1995 WBCCI Nor' by Nor' East Caravan" and [right] "Airstream Travel Trailers." Since the title of this chapter is "Airstream Pieces," we wanted to acknowledge that many Airstream owners and enthusiasts carry symbolic pieces of Airstreams around with them on their hats and clothing—in the form of fabric patches. Incidentally, the Nor' By Nor' East caravans have been popular national WBCCI sponsored caravans that have gone on the road some eight to ten times or more over the years. Each, $5-15.

Magazine Advertisement. Standard magazine paper, real color photo, full-page 9.75" x 12", by Dodge, in ROLLING STONE, October 31, 2002, page 147. Caption: "Dodge Durango. ... Grab Life By The Horns." The picture here illustrated a highly popular pattern for car, truck, and SUV manufacturers wishing to highlight the towing capabilities of their vehicles—to display only a small portion of the front of an Airstream trailer being pulled by one of their vehicles. We will see a number of these types of images in the coming pages. $5-10.

Advertising Postcard. Used, real color photo, 5.5" x 3.5", by Kampgrounds of America, #J3784, c. 1970s [postmark date illegible]. Half an Airstream is better than no Airstream at all. El Paso KOA was the campground publicized by this card, but there is no KOA listed in El Paso in the 2011-2012 KOA Directory. The postcard was sent by airmail from El Paso, Texas, to Albuquerque, New Mexico. $15-20.

Advertising Postcard. Used, real color photo, 5.5" x 3.5", by Free Lance Photo & Dexter Press, #75450-D, posted 1982. Only a small part of the upper area of an Airstream was visible in the top left hand corner of this three-image card. This scarce postcard advertised the Sunrise Shores Campground in Perry, Maine. The card was sent from Perry to Pascoag, Rhode Island. $10-15.

Advertising Postcard. Unused, real color photo, 5.5" x 3.5", by Linda Jo Fox, #771073, c. 1980s. Caption: "Rancho Campground" [in the Shenandoah Valley near New Market, Virginia]. The section of the Airstream revealed in the picture on this card was unusual—namely, part of the front and the lower section along the passenger side of the coach. But, there was no doubt that it was an Airstream parked just right of the center of the photograph. $10-15.

Advertising Postcard. Used [but not mailed], real black & white photo, 5.5" x 3.5", by Postcard Reproductions [although this is an authentic vintage card], #LTP-100, dated 1950 [handwritten note]. Caption: "Lakeside Trailer Park, Brownsville, Texas." The handwritten note on the reverse side remarked: "We stopped at this park for about a month … 1950." In the dark shadows of the trees to the right side of the picture was the unmistakable shape and appearance of part of the front of an Airstream. $20-25.

Advertising Postcard. Used, real color photo, 5.5" x 3.5", by L. E. Lang Publications, #170400, c. 1970s [posted from Mexico, but date illegible]. This three-image card promoted CC Camperland in Garden Grove, California, which the text on the back claimed to be "Orange County's finest overnight trailer park." And, most importantly, it was only "9 blocks south of Disneyland." A small L-shaped piece of an Airstream can be seen on the far left side of the picture. $10-15.

Advertising Postcard. Unused, real color photo, 5.5" x 3.5", by H. A. Pontier & Dexter Press, #35879, c. 1940s. Caption: "Ray Guy's Trailer Court … Fort Lee, N.J." New York City! The text on the back of the card pointed out that this RV park was just "1 mile south of New York City." Can you see the small segment of the Airstream trailer parked to the far right hand side of the picture? $20-25.

Advertising Brochure. Standard brochure cover & pages, real color photos, 8.5" x 11", by General Motors, #5530-84USA, 20 pages, dated 1984. Title: *GMC Trailering Guide*. What a picturesque RVing scene appeared on the front cover of this booklet—with just a tiny bit of an Airstream showing over the top of the truck. GM's slogan the "Mark of Excellence" seemed to fit Airstream's calibre, too. $20-25.

Advertising Brochure [underneath]. This image is the back cover of the brochure entitled *Airstream Trailer Fleet*, which was illustrated with a picture of its front cover early in this chapter. Here, on the back cover is the same classic image that is also shown on the accompanying belt buckle—namely, the iconic rear end of an Airstream. Why is Airstream's back end so memorable? For the brochure, $30-40.

Belt Buckle [on top]. Heavy metal, dark silver-gray finish, 2.5" x 2.5", by SMC LLC, unnumbered, copyright 2005. This clever and fun piece, illustrating what appears to be the back of an Airstream, even included its own humorous vanity license plate bearing the inscription "TRLRTRSH ... TRALER" [meaning trailer trash, and misspelling "trailer"]. Remember, it is the back end of the trailer that has been the first portion ever seen in person by millions of people as they have driven up behind Airstreams on the highways of the world. $30-40.

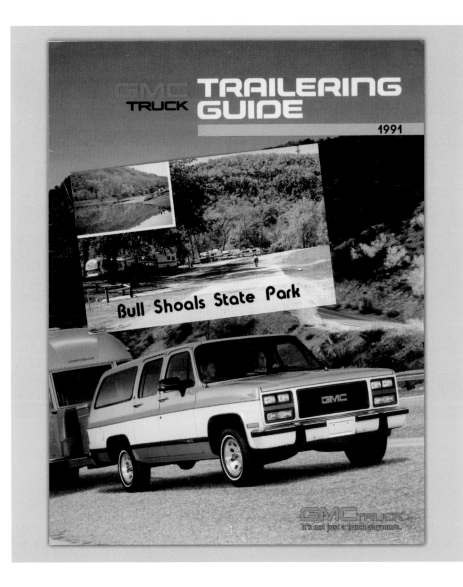

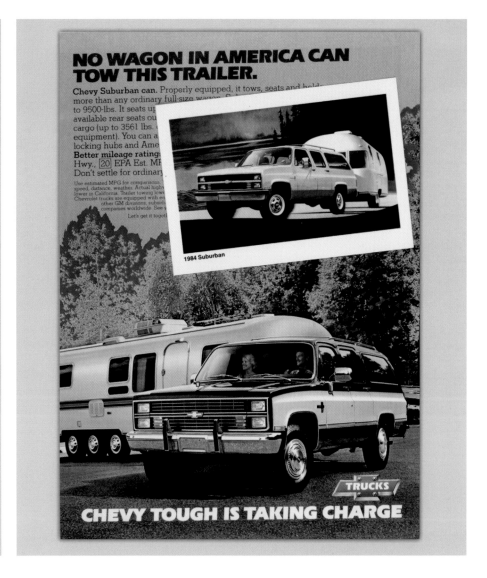

Advertising Brochure [underneath]. Standard brochure paper, real color photos, 8.25" x 11", by General Motors, #4846-91, 20 pages, dated 1991. Title: *GMC Truck Trailering Guide 1991*. Only a very small area on the front of the Airstream could be seen in tow behind the SUV in the picture on the cover of this booklet. There was also a picture showing a more complete Airstream being pulled by another GMC truck on page 3 of this brochure. $10-15.

Advertising Postcard [on top]. Used, real color photo, 5.5" x 3.5", by Lakeview Graphics & McGrew Color Graphics, #811012, posted 1984. Caption: "Bull Shoals State Park" [on the White River in Arkansas]. The senders wrote on the back of this card that the park was "a beautiful place" and they "planned to stay a week to do some trout fishing." The rear portion and some of the right side of a long Airstream trailer was visible under the trees at the extreme left edge of the picture. $10-15.

Magazine Advertisement [underneath]. Standard magazine paper, real color photo, 8" x 11", by General Motors, dated 1984. Caption: "No Wagon In America Can Tow This Trailer. ... Chevy Tough Is Taking Charge." The piece of the Airstream shown in this picture happened to include the area around the triple-axles—so we know this trailer was 30+ feet in length. No wonder this Chevy Suburban ad claimed no other wagon/truck could pull such a long and heavy trailer. $5-10.

Advertising Postcard [on top]. Unused, real color photo, 5.25" x 3.5", by General Motors, unnumbered, dated 1984. Caption: "1984 Suburban." What a handsome pair! The accompanying magazine advertisement was also dated 1984. It appears that an Airstream Argosy is in tow behind the Chevy in this picture. $15-20.

Only one wagon teams V-8 power, Turbo Hydra-Matic and 4-wheel drive. 'Jeep' Wagoneer

even park the Wagoneer with one finger.
V-8 engine, Turbo Hydra-Matic, 4-wheel drive...
that's a combination of options you'll only find in 'Jeep' Wagoneer. Test one soon at your 'Jeep' dealer's.

KAISER Jeep CORPORATION

All the power and twice the traction of ordinary family wagons

Magazine Advertisement [underneath]. Standard magazine paper, real color photo, 10" x 12", by General Motors, c. 1965. Caption: "Only one wagon teams V-8 power, Turbo Hydra-Matic and 4-wheel drive. 'Jeep' Wagoneer." This ad included a very small slice of an Airstream in tow. $5-10.

Advertising Postcard [on top]. Used, real color photo, 5.5" x 3.5", by O'Brien Color Studios, #15778, posted 1970. Red Coconut Trailer Park in Fort Myers Beach, Florida, was the campground pictured on this card. Notice how the coaches were parked along the beach, with their front ends close to the water [their tow cars would have been really close to the water, but would have been unhitched and moved off the beach and out of the way]. The RVers who sent this card wrote that they were staying "right here on the beach" and also commented in their message to a friend in Ohio: "These vacations are sure grand." A small section of a small Airstream could be seen in the middle of the group of trailers. $10-15.

Advertising Postcard. Used, real color photo, 5.5" x 3.5", by Gillian St. George & dynacolor graphics, unnumbered, posted 1997. This card publicized Breezy Pines RV Park on Big Pine Key, Florida. The authors actually stayed at this campground while on an RV trip in mid-December of 1997 and sent this postcard to family members in Illinois—so, the postcard served as our 1997 Christmas card. A small piece of an Airstream Argosy could be seen just left of center in the picture. $10-15.

Collector Postcard. Unused, real color photo, 6" x 4.25", by Airstream & Chronicle Books, unnumbered, copyright 2000. Caption: "Airstream Land Yacht, Florida, 1962." This picture was cleverly staged with people and beach accessories blocking much of the trailer. But, even though only a minority piece of the coach was visible, it was quite obvious that the trailer was an Airstream. Look at the mirror-like reflections against the exterior of this Airstream! $5-10.

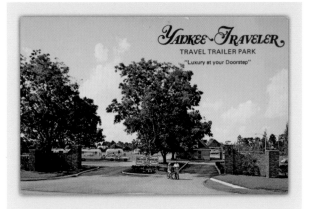

Advertising Postcard. Unused, real color photo, 5.5" x 3.5", by James Hess & Dexter Press, #69 & #49817-C, c. 1970s. Advertising Hickory Run Family Campground in Denver, Pennsylvania, in the Pennsylvania Dutch region. This card's photograph included part of an Airstream parked to its far right-center area. $10-15.

Advertising Postcard. Unused, real color photo, 5.5" x 3.5", by Jack Swenningsen, #114951, c. 1970s. Caption: "Yankee Traveler Travel Trailer Park … 'Luxury at Your Doorstep'." Can you see pieces of two different Airstreams in the picture on this card that publicized Yankee Traveler Park in Largo, Florida? The back of the card boasted of "200 beautiful spaces, deluxe atmosphere, and championship shuffleboard courts." $10-15.

Advertising Postcard. Unused, real color photo, 5.5" x 3.5", Stade Select Card & Curteichcolor, #9DK-676, c. 1960s. The campground pictured on this card was Pioneer Trailer Park on the Escanaba River between Escanaba and Gladstone, Michigan. A portion of the right side of an Airstream could be seen, including its well-recognized door-within-a-door side entry door design. $10-15.

Advertising Postcard. Used, real color photo, 5.5" x 3.5", by Tichnor Brothers, unnumbered, posted 1962. This well-known old card promoted Grindell's Ocean View Park in Dennis Port, Massachusetts. The sixth coach in the line of RVs along the beach was unquestionably an Airstream—although only a small bit of its rear section was visible. The senders' message on the back of the postcard, which was sent to family members in Massachusetts, announced that they were having a great time at this campground. $10-15.

Advertising Postcard. Unused, real color photo, 5.5" x 3.5", by Kentucky Post Card Company, #KPC-190, c. 1970s. This card advertised Riverside Camping at Beach Bend Park in Bowling Green, Kentucky. In the picture on its right hand side, the shiny front of an Airstream gleamed in the daylight, although the rest of the trailer was shaded by the trees. $10-15.

Advertising Postcard. Unused, real color photo, 5.5" x 3.5", by R. E. Drew & Dexter Press, #37847-C, c. 1970s-80s. Although there were three Airstreams visible in this picture, it was the small section of the top of the Airstream at the extreme right side of the photo that caused us to include this postcard. The card publicized Perry Trailer Park just off I-75 in Perry, Georgia. $10-15.

Advertising Postcard. Unused, real color photo, 5.5" x 3.5", by Bonita Jarvis, #128849, c. 1970s. This four-image card promoted Magic Valley Trailer Park in Weslaco, Texas, which was a huge RV park with some 600 sites—and offering such amenities as lighted shuffleboard, bingo [our favorite pastime], Spanish lessons, movies, therapeutic pool, billiards, square dancing, horseshoes, field trips, and more. Smaller and smaller pieces of six Airstream trailers could be seen down the line of parked RVs in the lower left hand photo. $10-15.

Magazine Advertisement [underneath]. Standard magazine paper, real color photo, 7.75" x 10.5", by Progressive Insurance, in *MOTORHOME*, September 2011, page 11. What a fun photo shot! This ad was for RV insurance. The people and the dog blocked most of the Airstream out of the picture, but notice that because Flo, the Progressive Insurance agent, was standing akimbo, the letters "RSTREAM" on the front of the trailer were visible next to her right arm. $5-10.

Advertising Postcard [on top]. Used, real color photo, 5.5" x 3.5", by Bonita Jarvis, #133372, posted 1980. Publicized by this three-image card was Paradise Park in McAllen, Texas. The handwritten message on the back was both sweet and cute. The senders of this postcard, who were staying at Paradise Park, began with the greeting "Dearest Mother," and they signed it "Usuns." They were on their way to join an RV caravan group [probably to travel to Mexico]. If you look closely, parts of the rear sections of two Airstreams could be seen parked at this campground. $10-15.

RV Miniatures. Three tiny Airstreams. On top is a heavy-metal Airstream toy or token for a key chain, about 1.75" x .5" x 1", and showing considerable detailing (such as its awning, roof and side panels, and side entry door). The middle Airstream is a tiny piece less than 1" long and .5" wide encased in a clear plastic paperweight cube that measures about 2" on each side. Again, the Airstream's detailing is remarkable for its tiny size. At the bottom is a small pewter RV set, composed of a tow vehicle less than 1" x .5" x .5", and an Airstream trailer less than 1.75" x .5" x .5"—both of which have nice details for their small sizes. Each, $20-25.

Chapter 6

AIRSTREAM *On the Road & Roadside*

The phrase travel trailer includes two operative words, one of which is "travel." That's what this chapter is about. More precisely, the chapter is about two distinct types of Airstream images. One setting for the images included here is the staged advertising picture of an Airstream either traveling down the highway or parked at the roadside. This pose has been a very popular and natural one for travel trailers because they are supposed to "travel" on the roadways of America.

The other setting is not staged. Sometimes photographs being taken for another purpose or focusing upon another subject will, quite by chance, capture additional items of interest to certain collectors. If a highway or roadside scene by happenstance also includes an image of an Airstream trailer, then this chance encounter is a blessing for those who collect Airstream pictures. Obviously, these accidental Airstream shots are quite difficult to collect because they occur purely by happenstance. We have managed to find some of these unusual treasures.

Thus, the images displayed in this chapter will show Airstreams as they travel about—as opposed to pictures of them settled into campgrounds or their other final destinations. These road and roadside settings have been important sources by which Airstream has been able to show the human side of Airstream trailering. So, we will see images of friends and families doing things together along the way and around their Airstreams, thereby promoting family unity and family values.

Especially in earlier decades, when amateur radio operation was even more popular, ham radio or amateur radio operators would often send postcards to one another in order to confirm and document their successful transmissions, and these cards were called QSL or CB radio cards. As a publicity tactic, Airstream issued a QSL card with blank spaces for amateur radio operators to fill in their individual call numbers and contact information. Page 69 shows one blank QSL card and one that has been filled-in.

Tourist Postcard. Used [but not mailed], real color photo, 5.5" x 3.5", by Murphy Brothers Press, #M7071, c. 1970s. Text on back of card: "Krome Avenue, a main boulevard in Homestead, Florida." Tourists wrote a message to themselves about the area on the back of the card, apparently as a way of tracking and remembering their travels. They even said they "got lost 2 or 3 times in this small city." This card is a personal favorite of ours because it demonstrates the way so many Americans have first been introduced to an Airstream—by driving up behind one on the highway and seeing the distinctive, shiny, aluminum, rounded, airplane-fuselage shape. Curiously, it was especially apropos that this postcard picture of the shiny rear-end of an Airstream was captured on "Krome" Avenue. Like another card on these pages, this one also exemplifies a true "roadside" category find, in which the Airstream got into the picture quite by chance. $20-25.

Advertising Postcard. Unused, real color photo, large 7" x 5.25", by Airstream, unnumbered, c. 1960s. Caption: "Airstream Land Yachting—The Better Way To Travel." The impressive picture on this card showed an Airstream parked in a scenic turnout along a coastline with a lighthouse in the distant background. Compare the other similar images on the postcards on this page. $30-40.

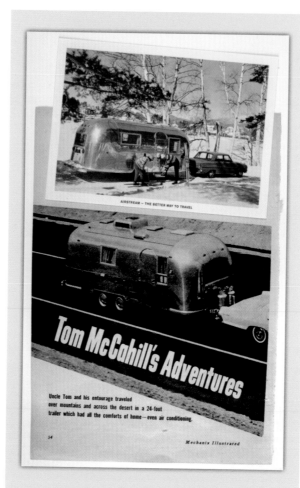

Advertising Postcard. Unused, real color photo, large 7" x 5.25", by Airstream, unnumbered, c. 1960s-70s. Caption: "Airstream Land Yachting—The Better Way To Travel." No other travel trailer looks so good and so distinctive at night! Just the smallest amount of light can set the Airstream aglow. Here, a pair of Airstreams and their tow cars were parked along a curb in Washington, D.C. $20-25.

Organization Pennant. Triangular nylon fabric, tri-color graphics, 18" x 12", by Annin Nyl-Glo, unnumbered, c. 1980s-90s. Inscription: "Wally Byam Caravan Club International C.B. Radio Club." The WBCCI family includes a number of associated organizations, including its CB Radio Club of amateur or ham radio enthusiasts. This simple and impressive pennant is the club banner and proudly flies over many Airstream trailers. For this vintage version, $20-25.

Collector Postcard [on top]. Unused, real color photo, 6" x 4.25", by Airstream & Chronicle Books, copyright 2000. Caption: "Airstream—The Better Way To Travel." It appeared that Airstream did not want to leave anyone out of its advertising audience. So, here was the appeal to those hearty souls who snow ski, ice skate, and toboggan. $5-10.

Magazine Article [underneath]. Standard magazine paper, real black & white photo, 6.5" x 9.25", in *MECHANIX ILLUSTRATED*, "Tom McCahill's Adventures," by Tom McCahill, July 1965, page 54. Here, on the cover page of this article, was a perfectly staged and exactly framed picture of a 24-foot Airstream gliding down the highway. Notice that the article summary mentioned the trailer "had all the comforts of home—even air conditioning." Remember, it was 1965. For the article, $5-10.

Advertising Postcard. Unused, real color photo, large 7" x 5.25", by Airstream, unnumbered, c. 1960s. Caption: "Airstream Land Yachting—The Better Way To Travel." Pre-printed on the back of this card was the sender's name and address—Mann's Trailer Sales of Normal, Illinois. The picturesque and enticing scene on this postcard showed a mini-caravan of three Airstreams at dusk on a roadside with a lake and mountains in the background. It really was the better way to travel! $30-40.

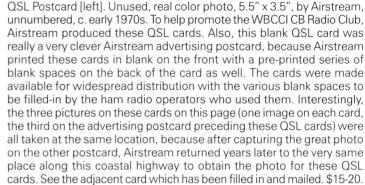

QSL Postcard [left]. Unused, real color photo, 5.5" x 3.5", by Airstream, unnumbered, c. early 1970s. To help promote the WBCCI CB Radio Club, Airstream produced these QSL cards. Also, this blank QSL card was really a very clever Airstream advertising postcard, because Airstream printed these cards in blank on the front with a pre-printed series of blank spaces on the back of the card as well. The cards were made available for widespread distribution with the various blank spaces to be filled-in by the ham radio operators who used them. Interestingly, the three pictures on these cards on this page (one image on each card, the third on the advertising postcard preceding these QSL cards) were all taken at the same location, because after capturing the great photo on the other postcard, Airstream returned years later to the very same place along this coastal highway to obtain the photo for these QSL cards. See the adjacent card which has been filled in and mailed. $15-20.

QSL Postcard [right]. Used, real color photo, 5.5" x 3.5", by Airstream, unnumbered, posted 1972. Caption: "W3GD – K4GD [along with the ham radio operator's name and street addresses—redacted for privacy reasons] Ulysses, Pa. 16948 ... Lady Lake, Fl. 32659." This amateur radio or CB card and Airstream advertising card was sent from a radio operator in Pennsylvania to a fellow amateur operator in Tennessee, to confirm multiple transmissions between them in 1971-72. Obviously, the picture on this card is identical to the accompanying blank QSL card, and shows an Airstream in the same coastal setting as appears on the other cards on this page. $15-20.

Tourist Postcard. Unused, real color photo, 5.5" x 3.5", by New Process Colorcard & A. V. Pollard, #7C-K229, c. 1950s. This marvelous card bears the description on its reverse side: "Car line-up for ferry departure, Beacon Avenue, Sidney, B.C." Although the ferry dock was in British Columbia, Canada, the postcard was made in the USA. Three vintage travel trailers were shown in the picture, and the last one in line was a mint-condition Airstream towed by a handsome sedan complete with a boat on its roof. This card was a great "roadside" category find—a picture postcard which by happenstance captured the image of an Airstream. $25-50.

AIRSTREAM LAND YACHTING—THE BETTER WAY TO TRAVEL

Advertising Postcard. Unused, real color photo, large 7" x 5.25", by Airstream, unnumbered, c. 1960s. Caption: "Airstream Land Yachting—The Better Way To Travel." Once again, this ad was exceptionally inviting and effective, with the Airstream well off the beaten path. Even though the Airstream occupied such a small portion of the picture on this card, the image was a masterful piece of Airstream advertising. Admittedly, this large card was about 50% larger than the standard size postcard, so that the Airstream was as big as it would have been on a smaller card. $20-25.

AIRSTREAM LAND YACHTING—THE BETTER WAY TO TRAVEL

Advertising Postcard. Unused, real color photo, large 7" x 5.25", by Airstream, unnumbered, c. 1960s. Caption: "Airstream Land Yachting—The Better Way To Travel." Again, the Airstream in this picture had found its way into rugged Western terrain [although on nice flat pavement]. This stunning Airstream card is certainly a highly sought postcard, partly because it featured Native Americans in it. The text on the back of the card suggested that people "blaze a trail deep into Indian country." And, it went on to say: "When you go Airstream, adventure will find you! ... Your ports of call are anywhere you decide, your imagination is your only itinerary." It certainly was the better way to experience history and geography! $25-50.

Magazine Advertisement [underneath]. Standard magazine paper, multi-color graphic, 8" x 11", by American Motors, in *PLAYBOY*, 1974. Caption: "Jeep Wagoneer ... The Ultimate in 4-wheel drive." Over the decades, as we have seen in earlier chapters, several automobile manufacturers developed handsome advertisements with their cars towing Airstream trailers. This decision by some carmakers was a savvy one, because any car looks good in front of an Airstream and because Airstream is a lightweight trailer that can be more easily towed than so many other trailer brands. Notice how effortlessly the Jeep seemed to pull the Airstream along the unpaved mountain road in this colorful scene. $5-10.

Advertising Postcard [on top]. Unused, real color photo, 5.5" x 3.5", by Pioneer Advertising Promotions, #12975-C, c. 1960s. Caption: "Phifer Wire Products" [of Tuscaloosa, Alabama]. The text on the back of this postcard suggested: "See America Best Through Phifer Sunscreen," because this three-image card advertised a company that manufactured aluminum-clad sunscreens for RVs. Incidentally, the pictured Airstream certainly was a very finely polished coach. $15-20.

Magazine Advertisement [underneath]. Standard magazine paper, real black & white photo, 6" x 9", by Airstream, c. 1970s. Caption: "Discover Real Travel Adventure!" The two pictures in this ad and on the adjacent card showed two Airstreams—one on the road, and one on the roadside. $5-10.

Tourist Postcard [on top]. Unused, real color photo, 5.5" x 3.5", by Petley Studios, #P63443, c. 1960s. Caption: "4 Corners ... Arizona, Utah, Colorado, New Mexico." It is, according to the text on the reverse side of the card, "the only spot in the United States where four states meet at a common corner." Hence, on the day this photograph was taken, a unique place was host to a unique travel trailer—the Airstream. $20-25.

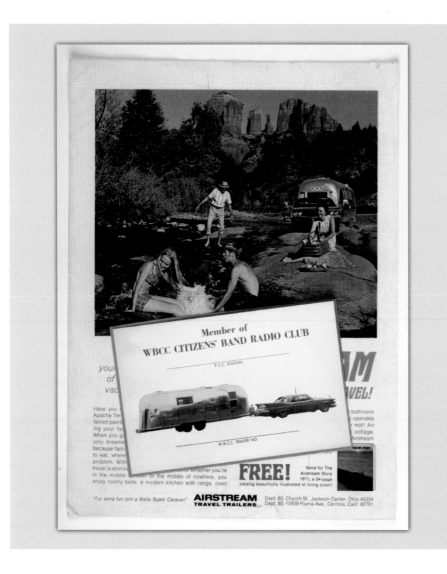

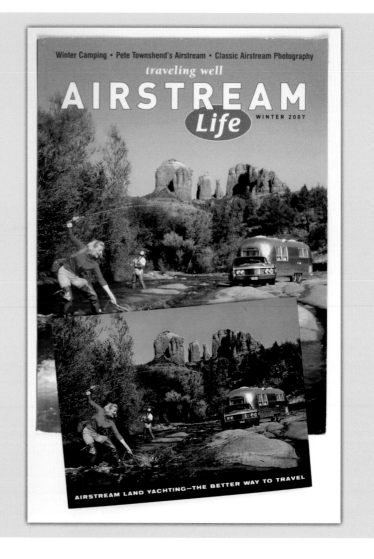

Magazine Advertisement [underneath]. Back cover of magazine on heavy paper, real color photo, 8" x 11", by Airstream, dated 1971. Caption: "Fulfill your dreams of family vacations—Go Airstream—The better way to travel!" With Airstreams, the roads on which they travel may be fairly remote and primitive, as in this picture. But, the wilderness scene here certainly appeared to be inviting. Notice that the scenic backdrop for this advertisement was the identical one for the photographs on the right. $5-10.

QSL Postcard [on top]. Unused, real black & white photo, 5.5" x 3.5", no maker, unnumbered, c. 1960s. Caption: "Member of WBCC [Wally Byam Caravan Club] Citizens' Band Radio Club." Appropriately, the picture on this postcard displayed a long tandem-axle Airstream (like the one in the adjacent magazine ad) and tow car with a distinctive radio antenna. The front and back of this very scarce card were pre-printed with blank spaces for use by various amateur radio operators. $25-50.

Magazine Cover [underneath]. Heavy magazine cover paper, real color photo, 8" x 11", in *AIRSTREAM LIFE*, Winter 2007. What a fun image, originally taken about 1970. The tow car and Airstream on this magazine cover seemed to be just a little off-road in this scene. This picture showed a camping couple happily fishing a Western stream with dramatic desert rock formations in the background. And, look at the photo on the accompanying postcard. For this issue of the magazine, $10-15.

Advertising Postcard [on top]. Unused, real color photo, large 7" x 5.25", by Airstream, unnumbered, c. 1970s. Caption: "Airstream Land Yachting—The Better Way To Travel." This picture is one of the better known and recognized Airstream images—and, Airstream has displayed savvy business sense by re-using this effective image. $30-40.

ALOHA!

GO WHERE THE COWBOYS GO

ROAD TRIP, 1963

Collector Postcard. Unused, real color photo, 6" x 4.25", by Airstream, unnumbered, copyright 2000 [c. 1960s era photo]. Caption: "Go Where The Cowboys Go." The pictures on this page and several of the photos on the next few pages showed family scenes—what today would be called promoting "family values." $5-10.

Collector Postcard. Unused, real color photo, 6" x 4.25", by Airstream, unnumbered, copyright 2000. Caption: "Road Trip, 1963." Although these two trailers appeared to be traveling side-by-side down the highway, the picture was obviously posed to show both the contrast in sizes between the two Airstreams and the upscale quality of the Airstreams [as one was even pulled by a Lincoln Continental]. $5-10.

AIRSTREAM – YOUR PASSPORT TO UNLIMITED TRAVEL ADVENTURE

KING OF THE ROAD

Collector Postcard. Unused, real color photo, 6" x 4.25", by Airstream & Chronicle Books, unnumbered, copyright 2000 [c. 1960s era picture]. Caption: "Aloha!" If the scene in this photo was really Hawaii, that set of circumstances would have been highly unusual—because there have never been many RVs of any kind in Hawaii (for a lot of reasons). But, it was possible, and if any trailer company were likely to have gone to the islands for publicity purposes, it would have been Airstream. $5-10.

Collector Postcard. Unused, real color photo, 6" x 4.25", by Airstream, unnumbered, copyright 2000 [c. 1960s era photo]. Caption: "Airstream—Your Passport To Unlimited Travel Adventure." Several old and new Airstream publicity pictures have utilized the technique of brightly lighting the inside of the trailer in a night-time setting—with the dramatic effect achieved in this photo. $5-10.

Collector Postcard. Unused, real color photo, 6" x 4.25", by Airstream, unnumbered, copyright 2000. Caption: "King of the Road." The picture here was probably taken in the early 1960s, and the tow car and trailer certainly looked grand. $5-10.

Magazine Advertisement [underneath]. Standard magazine paper, real color photo, 6" x 9", by Chevrolet, in *POPULAR MECHANICS*, November 1972, page 177. Caption: "New 1973 Chevrolet Suburban. ... Moves up to 14,000 lbs. ... Building a better way to see the U.S.A." In the picture in this ad, the Chevy SUV and the Airstream on the upward sloping wilderness roadway seemed made for one another. $5-10.

QSL Card [on top]. Unused, real black & white photo, 5.25" x 3.25", no maker, unnumbered, c. 1960s. Caption: "KPK2061 ... Walter & Hazel [surname and street address redacted for privacy reasons] ... Gary, Indiana." What a great QSL card, with a perfectly framed picture of the ham radio couple's Airstream trailer. It is unusual for QSL cards to illustrate RVs, and quite unusual for Airstreams to appear. $40-50.

Magazine Advertisement. Standard magazine cover paper, real color photo, 7.75" x 11", by Airstream, in *AIRSTREAM LIFE*, Fall 2009. Caption: "Nights in shining armor." Wow! This stunning ad, which appeared on the magazine's inside back cover, exemplified why it has been said, "There is sophistication in simplicity." The simple picture is fantastic, and the simple text of the advertisement is also eloquent: "Adventures during the day; comfort at night; life with Airstream." Of course, the knight in shining armor is typically associated with the romantic hero, in keeping with the family scenes often included in Airstream advertising. This particular ad is being regularly re-run by Airstream, as it should be. $5-10.

Advertising Postcard. Unused, real color photo, large 7" x 5.25", by Airstream, unnumbered, c. 1960s. Caption: "Airstream Land Yachting—The Better Way To Travel." This nostalgic family scene was in keeping with the images on the next few Airstream pieces shown on the coming pages—each of which fostered Airstream's message that romance and memories come with Airstream trailering, and in this particular instance, generation after generation. $30-40.

Publicity Postcard. Unused, real color photo, 5.5" x 3.5", by Mike Roberts & CBS Card Service, #C31593, c. 1970s. This card promoted the Reelfoot Lake area, which lies between Tiptonville and Samburg in the northwestern part of Tennessee. The lake is known for its historic cypress tree formations and its close similarity to a swamp or bayou. Not surprisingly, a long Airstream trailer just happened to have stopped near the shoreline when this photograph was taken. $10-15.

Magazine Advertisement. Standard magazine paper, real black & white photo, 6.5" x 4.5", by Airstream, 1967. Caption: "Discover real travel adventure." This picture showed another setting with horses and riders and an Airstream. It was quite effectively tempting people with the allure of the great outdoors. $5-10.

Collector Postcard. Unused, real color photo, 6" x 4.25", by Airstream & Chronicle Books, unnumbered, copyright 2000. Caption: "Romance Is Always In Season." This card, and the previous one, illustrated again one of the themes Airstream has been fond of promoting—the romantic feature of trailering in an Airstream. Or perhaps, to put it another way, a family that Airstreams together, stays together. $5-10.

Advertising Postcard. Unused, real color photo, large 7" x 5.25", by Airstream, unnumbered, c. 1960s. Caption: "Airstream Land Yachting—The Better Way To Travel." The picture on this card was simply a nice, serene setting—with a campfire, horses for riding, and three Airstreams parked in a half-circle together. See the similar picture in the adjacent magazine advertisement as well. $20-25.

Magazine Advertisement. Standard magazine paper, real black & white photo, 6.5" x 4.5", by Airstream, c. 1970s. Caption: "Discover Real Travel Adventure!" Can you see the similarities between the pictures in this ad and the adjacent postcard? Both scenes show Airstreamers along their route, stopping for a bite of lunch. $5-10.

Holiday Ornament. Standard ornament glass, hand-painted shiny silver & black graphics, 5.5" x 2.5" x 3.5", by Jennifer Ellsworth Landmarks, unnumbered, 2006. This ornament is the third one by Jennifer Ellsworth to appear in this book, because they are so exceptionally well-done and so highly prized. This piece illustrates a contemporary Airstream, again including wonderful structural details—like the vent panels, side entry door, warning lights, front and rear roof panels, hubcaps, and more. The ornament was hand-blown and hand-painted in Poland. $40-50.

Collector Postcard. Unused, real black & white photo, 6" x 4.25", by Airstream, unnumbered, copyright 2000 [c. 1970s era photo]. Caption: "Romance Is Always In Season." Of course, when scenes were staged for Airstream publicity pictures, more than one photograph was taken, and more than one from the same photo shoot may have been used in advertising. The photo on this card and the photo on the adjacent magazine advertisement illustrate the point. You can readily tell that the cars, the sand dunes, and the Airstreams in the image on page 75 were the same. $5-10.

RV Cookbook [underneath]. Standard spiral-bound book covers & paper, two-color graphics, 6.5" x 9.5", by WBCCI Washington Unit, unnumbered, 130 pages, c. 1970s. Title: *Recipes For Land And Sea Cruising.* Also known as *Your Travelin' Cookbook*, this spiral-bound community-based book was prepared by Airstreamers in the Washington Unit of WBCCI living at Washington Land Yacht Haven in Lacey, Washington. All of the many recipes included are handwritten in long hand. We decided to include the cookbook here because we know from experience that, when RVers and their RVs are stopped along the highways in rest areas, parking lots, and the like, they very often have stopped in order to prepare and eat a meal. $10-15.

Belt Buckle [on top]. Heavy metal, 3-D multi-color graphics, 3" x 2.5", no maker, unnumbered, c. 1990s-2000s. Inscription: "Happy Trails." This distinctive and handsome buckle is highly detailed, with numerous raised features on the front, and even on its reverse side [where two raised eagles serve as the support piece and the catch-pin for the buckle mechanism]. A long, three-axle Airstream Land Yacht parked in a mountain setting was the centerpiece for the design. $20-25.

Chapter 7

AIRSTREAM Parks & Rallies

Among Wally Byam's most successful strokes of genius was his promotion of deep customer loyalty to Airstream. He encouraged Airstream owners to become part of an extended Airstream family—to travel in Airstream exclusive caravans, to attend Airstream only rallies, and to stay at Airstream exclusive parks. Some might call him an Airstream snob, but others would call him a savvy businessman. Of course, Airstream has also undertaken all of the more common types of customer goodwill activities—such as providing a network for parts and service, publishing magazines and newsletters, forming clubs and organizations, and producing memorabilia.

Other RV brands have even copied some of the methods Wally Byam introduced to foster customer loyalty to Airstream. Rallies are commonly held for owners of some other brands of RVs, and several other RV brands have published magazines and newsletters for their owners. Yet, no other RV brand has come even close to rivaling Airstream's success in promoting high levels of owner loyalty.

This chapter displays only a small sampling of the wide array of collectibles that have been created to remember the Airstream parks and rallies. The postcards and memorabilia commemorating the various Airstream rallies, especially the big annual international ones, have become quite collectible. And among those rally collectibles, the aerial photographs of the large rallies are especially desirable, particularly the vintage postcards for the earlier years of the Airstream rallies.

The Airstream rally tradition lives on, over fifty years later. More than any other manufacturer or organization in the history of RVing, Airstream has spawned lasting traditions and has contributed significantly to the growth of RVing. Consider the domestic and international caravans; the national, regional, and local rallies; the membership clubs and publications; the exclusive campgrounds; and, the excellence and longevity of its coaches. These are some of the reasons that have contributed to Airstream's status as the oldest and longest operating RV manufacturer.

Rally Mugs. Two collectible ceramic handled cups, multi-color graphics, 3" diameter x 3.5" tall, by WBCC Kentucky Unit, unnumbered, c. 1971. Inscription: "[1961 – 1971 …] Kentucky Unit … Wally Byam Caravan Club … Kentucky Derby Rally." The same, but different. The only discernible difference between these collector mugs is that the one to the left side has the dates "1961-1971" applied to it, while the other piece does not. These mugs commemorated the Airstream rallies held in Louisville. As we will see, many types of collectibles have been produced to commemorate WBCCI caravans and rallies. Incidentally, Louisville was the site of the 19th International WBCCI Rally in 1976, which had the largest attendance of all of the 50+ annual international rallies (with 4493 registrants). Each, $15-20.

There are several Airstream parks around the country—including Highland Haven Airstream Park in Copper Hill, Virginia; Land Yacht Harbor in Melbourne, Florida; Minnesota Airstream Park in Clear Lake, Minnesota; North Texas Airstream Community in Hillsboro, Texas; Penn Wood Airstream Park near Clarion, Pennsylvania; Tennessee Cumberland Plateau Campground in Crossville, Tennessee; and, Washington Land Yacht Harbor in Lacey, Washington.

Advertising Postcard. Used, real color photo, 5.5" x 3.5", by Wasman Photography, #150417, posted 1978. This scarce card promoted the Recreational Vehicle Park in Eustis, Florida, and the text on the back of the card pointed out that the campground was "a full-service rally park." Coincidently [or maybe not], a major Airstream rally was shown in progress when the publicity picture was taken [see the adjacent card as well]. The card was sent by a lady staying at this RV park to a friend in Rogersville, Tennessee. $20-25.

Tourist Postcard. Unused, real color photo, 5.5" x 3.5", by Kelley's Studio, #ICS-107262, c. 1960s-70s. This card promoted "Wally Byam Caravan Club." The text on the reverse side of the postcard pointed out: "The nationally known Club of travelers are parked at Sugarcreek, Ohio. The Little Switzerland of Ohio. Each year the 3rd Fri. and Sat. of September Sugarcreek has what has become famous … a Swiss Cheese Festival." This Swiss Festival rally is among the national rallies sponsored by WBCCI. This postcard and its handsome rally picture have become well-known to Airstream memorabilia collectors. $10-15.

Advertising Postcard. Unused, real color photo, 5.5" x 3.5", by Wasman Photography, #150418, c. 1970s. Like the neighboring card, this postcard publicized Recreational Vehicle Park in Eustis, Florida, and neither card mentioned that an Airstream rally was pictured! $20-25.

Advertising Postcard. Unused, real color aerial photo, by Flagler Fotoshop, #S15265, dated 1958. This hard-to-find card publicized Coral Sands Trailer Park & Motel in Key Largo, Florida. The text on the reverse side of the postcard noted: "Photo taken during annual mid-winter airstream trailer rally 1958" [no capital A on Airstream in original!]. $20-25.

Tourist Postcard [underneath]. Unused, real black & white aerial photo, 5.5" x 3.5", by L. L. Cook Company, unnumbered, dated 1963. Caption: "6th International Rally ... Bemidji, Minn. ... 1963." $20-25.

Bolo Tie Medallions [on top]. Two metal & hard plastic circular crests, multi-color graphics, 1.5" diameter, by WBCCI, unnumbered, dated 1983 [left] & 1991 [right]. Inscriptions: "Int'l WBCCI Rally ... 1983 ... Duluth, MN" [left]. "Northern Comfort ... WBCCI ... Duluth ... 1991" [right]. Each, $10-15.

Collector Postcard. Unused, real black & white photo, 6" x 4.25", by Airstream & Chronicle Books, unnumbered, copyright 2000. Caption: "Palm Springs Airstream Rally, 1958." $5-10.

Tourist Postcard. Used, real black & white aerial photo, 5.5" x 3.5", no maker, unnumbered, dated & posted 1962. Caption: "5th International Rally ... Auburn, Wash. ... 1962." This scarce card was sent from Auburn by a fellow attending the rally to a friend in Ohio, and he wrote in his message on the back of the postcard that there were "1750 trailers here." This rally was one at which the organizers were able to form the coaches in attendance into a very large wagon wheel. $30-40.

Tourist Postcard. Unused, real black & white aerial photo, 5.5" x 3.5", by Photo Group, unnumbered, dated 1964. Text on the back of card: "Wally Byam Caravan Club ... 7th International Rally ... Princeton, New Jersey ... June 22 to July 5, 1964." Again, the wheel pattern [though actually more of an oblong shape] was utilized to park the Airstreams in attendance. $20-25.

Tourist Postcard [underneath]. Unused, real black & white aerial photo, 5.5" x 3.5", by Kermode [Canada], unnumbered, dated 1962. Caption: "Wally Byam Caravan, Vernon, B.C. – July 1962." Note the pattern of the coaches parked at this rally in British Columbia, Canada. Starting with Wally Byam's first international caravan in about 1951 to Mexico, he had the trailers park whenever possible in a wagon wheel design, which he felt was both the best pattern for democratic decision-making by the caravan members and the easiest pattern for the parking and departure of the trailers. $30-40.

Bolo Tie Medallion [on top]. Heavy metal & hard plastic circular design, multi-color graphics, 1.5" diameter, by WBCCI, unnumbered ["Made in Korea" on back], dated 1993. Inscription: "Prairie Safari ... Bismarck-Mandan ... North Dakota ... WBCCI 1993." This scarce and impressive medallion included a sculptured bison at its center. $15-20.

PALM SPRINGS AIRSTREAM RALLY, 1958

Collector Postcard [underneath]. Unused, real black & white photo, 6" x 4.25", by Airstream & Chronicle Books, unnumbered, copyright 2000. Caption: "Palm Springs Airstream Rally, 1958." The year 1958 was also the year of the first Wally Byam Caravan Club International Rally, held that year in Bull Shoals, Arkansas. These legendary international rallies have been held annually for over 50 years! $5-10.

Collector Medallions [on top]. Two circular metal crests [bolo tie clasp—left; lapel pin—right], multi-color graphics, 1.75" diameter—left & 1" diameter—right, by WBCCI, unnumbered, dated 1998. Inscription: "41st International Rally ... Boise, ID ... WBCCI 1998." The graphic design of these two different-sized medallions was identical, and included the state capitol building and a hot air balloon. Each, $10-15.

Tourist Postcard [underneath]. Used, real black & white aerial photo, by Haines Studio, unnumbered, dated & posted 1966. Text on back of card: "Wally Byam Caravan Club International ... 9th International Rally ... Cadillac, Michigan ... June 28 to July 5, 1966." Handwritten message from a couple attending the rally, sent from Cadillac to friends in Fort Worth, Texas: "Hi. Up here in the great gathering. Sure lots of trailers from all over. Good to see old friends again." Notice that most of the RVs parked at "the great gathering" were positioned in the wagon wheel formation, although it appears there were so many that a large group of trailers had to be parked in an overflow area in straight rows to the left side of the picture. $20-25.

Bolo Tie Medallion [on top]. Metal oblong crest, multi-color graphics, large 2.25" x 1.75", by WBCCI, unnumbered, dated 2004. Inscription: "WBCCI 2004 ... Great Lakes ... Great Times ... Great City ... Lansing [Michigan] ... 47th International Rally." Stunning graphic! Not surprisingly, the crest featured an early Ford automobile, since nearby Detroit is the automotive center of the USA. $15-20.

Tourist Postcard. Unused, real black & white aerial photo, 5.5" x 3.25", by The Easel, unnumbered, dated 1965. Reverse side text: "Wally Byam Caravan International ... 8th Rally ... 1965 ... Laramie, Wyoming." The aerial picture turned out to be a bit too dark, but it still showed the immensity of the attendance at this rally. $10-15.

Tourist Postcard. Unused, real black & white aerial photo, 5.5" x 3.5", no maker, unnumbered, dated 1967. Caption: "Airstream Northeast Rally ... May 26-28, 1967 ... Bloomsburg, Pennsylvania." The picture on this card was much too dark. $10-15.

Tourist Postcard. Unused, real black & white aerial photo, 5.5" x 3.5", no maker, unnumbered, dated 1967. Caption: "Airstream Northwest Rally ... Aug. 25-27, 1967 ... Gresham, Oregon." The picture on this card was a little dark. $15-20.

Advertising Postcard [underneath]. Unused, real color photo, 5.5" x 3.5", by Conover Printing, #28073, dated 1966. This card advertised Old Dutch Mill Park, a campground in "Dutch country" in Kutztown, Pennsylvania, and the picture on the postcard was taken during a local Airstream rally. The text on the back of the postcard read, in part: "View of the Wally Byam Air Stream Trailer Rally, 1966." Did you notice the card's variation on the name Airstream? $20-25.

Bolo Tie Medallion [on top]. Heavy metal & hard plastic circular crest, tri-color graphics, 1.75" diameter, no maker, unnumbered, dated 1986. Inscription: "Great Treasureland Getaway ... 1986 ... Boise ... Idaho." Simple and sophisticated! $15-20.

Fabric Patches. Two tight-weave circular patches, multi-color graphics, 3.5" diameter [left] & 3" diameter [right], by WBCCI, unnumbered, dated 1997 [left] & 1998 [right]. Inscriptions: "1997 WBCCI International Rally ... 40 Year ... Huntsville ... Alabama" [left]. "41st International Rally ... Boise, ID ... WBCCI 1998" [right]. Both patches showed detailed and thoughtful graphic design. Each, $5-10.

Tourist Postcard [underneath]. Unused, real color aerial photo, large 7" x 5.25", no maker, unnumbered, dated 1967. Text on reverse side of card: "Over 10,000 Wally Byam Caravan Club Members in over 3,000 Airstream Travel Trailers enjoying their 10th International Rally in beautiful Sonoma County near Santa Rosa, California, June 27 thru July 4, 1967." It is somewhat difficult to see the Airstream coaches against the concrete airport pavement on which they were parked in the picture on this card, but the card has nevertheless become a scarce collectible. $25-50.

Bolo Tie Medallion [on top]. Heavy metal & hard plastic circular crest, multi-color graphics, 1.75" diameter, by WBCCI, unnumbered ["Made in Korea" on back], dated 1988. Inscription: "Space Age Odyssey ... wbcci ... 88 ... Huntsville" [Alabama]. The city of Huntsville is an important hub in aeronautics and space research and development. The fun graphic on this nice medallion showed an astronaut in a space suit seated on a planet or moon, having already planted the US flag there. $15-20.

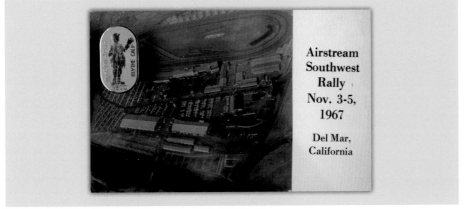

Tourist Postcard [underneath]. Unused, real black & white aerial photo, 5.25" x 3.5", no maker, unnumbered, dated 1967. Caption: "Airstream Southwest Rally ... Nov. 3-5, 1967 ... Del Mar, California." The picture on this card was a bit too light. $10-15.

Rally Collector Pin [on top]. Metal oblong crest with push-pin & clasp, two-color graphic, small .75" x 1.25", by WBCCI, unnumbered, c. 1980s-90s. Caption: "Hobo Rally ... WBCCI ... Blythe, Calif." The Hobo Rally is a national WBCCI rally. This handsome lapel pin was produced in Airstream-blue and gold colors, with the image of a hobo at its center. $10-15.

Tourist Postcard [underneath]. Used, real black & white aerial photo, 5.25" x 3.5", no maker, unnumbered, dated 1968. Caption: "Airstream Northeast Rally ... May 30 – June 2, 1968 ... Bloomsburg, Pa." The card was mailed to Clyde, Pennsylvania. $15-20.

Bolo Tie Medallion [on top]. Metal rectangular crest, multi-color graphics, large 1.75" x 2.5", by WBCCI, unnumbered, dated 2003. Inscription: "The Hills Are Alive In Vermont ... Burlington ... WBCCI ... 2003 ... 46th International Rally." This unusual and fun medallion was made large and rectangular in order to fit a sizable map of Vermont into its graphic design. $15-20.

Tourist Postcard. Used, real black & white aerial photo, 5.25" x 3.5", no maker, unnumbered, dated & posted 1968. Caption: "Airstream Southeastern Rally ... Feb. 9-11, 1968 ... West Palm Beach, Florida." Sometimes the quality of the aerial pictures on these rally cards is not the most crisp. This postcard was sent a week after the rally from Fort Myers, Florida, to Canton, Ohio. The card was sent by a couple who had attended the rally and who wrote in their message on the back of the card that there had been 1700 trailers at the West Palm Beach rally. $10-15.

Tourist Postcard [underneath]. Unused, real black & white aerial photo, 5.5" x 3.5", no maker, unnumbered, 1970. Text on the reverse side of card: "Wally Byam Caravan Club International Inc. ... 13th International Rally ... Hershey, Pennsylvania ... 'Chocolate Town, U.S.A.'" $10-15.

Key Chain Medallion [on top]. Thick metal, two-sided circular crest with raised print & graphics, 1.25" diameter, by WBCCI, unnumbered, 1970. Inscription: "WBCCI ... 13th Int'l Rally ... Hershey, Penna" on front, with raised image of tandem-axle Airstream parked in wilderness setting on back. $20-25.

Airstream Northeast Rally May 30-June 1, 1969
Bloomsburg, Pa.

Tourist Postcard. Unused, real black & white aerial photo, 5.25" x 3.5", no maker, unnumbered, dated 1969. Caption: "Airstream Northeast Rally ... May 30 – June 1, 1969 ... Bloomsburg, Pa." $15-20.

Tourist Postcard. Unused, real black & white aerial photo, 5.5" x 3.5", by Dan Stivers, unnumbered, dated 1970. Text on reverse side: "Airstream Rally 1970 ... Sarasota, Florida." $15-20.

12TH INTERNATIONAL RALLY
Wally Byam Caravan Club
LARAMIE, WYOMING 1969

Tourist Postcard [underneath]. Unused, real black & white aerial photo, 5.25" x 4.25", by Ludwig Photo Enterprises, unnumbered, dated 1969. Caption: "12th International Rally ... Wally Byam Caravan Club ... Laramie, Wyoming 1969." Notice how nicely this card was designed with its white border and the classic image of globetrotter Wally Byam posed, appropriately, in front of a globe. $20-25.

Collector Medallions [on top]. Two metal & hard plastic circular crests, multi-color graphics, 1.75" diameter [left] & 1" diameter [right], by WBCCI, unnumbered, dated 1997. Inscription: "1997 WBCCI International Rally ... 40 Year ... Huntsville ... Alabama." The larger medallion on the left is the clasp for a bolo tie, while the smaller crest to the right is a lapel pin—both having the identical graphic design. Each, $10-15.

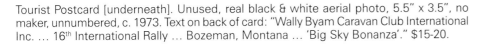

Tourist Postcard [underneath]. Unused, real black & white aerial photo, 5.5" x 3.5", no maker, unnumbered, c. 1973. Text on back of card: "Wally Byam Caravan Club International Inc. ... 16th International Rally ... Bozeman, Montana ... 'Big Sky Bonanza'." $15-20.

Bolo Tie Medallion [on top]. Heavy metal & hard plastic circular crest, multi-color graphics, 1.75" diameter, by WBCCI, unnumbered, dated 2000. Inscription: "WBCCI ... 2000 ... 43rd International Rally ... Bismarck, ND." This bright and impressive medallion sported a stylized buffalo head at its center. $15-20.

Tourist Postcard [underneath]. Unused, real black & white aerial photo, small 5" x 3", no maker, unnumbered, 1974. Text on reverse side: "Wally Byam Caravan Club International Inc. ... 17th International Rally ... Athletic & Convocation Center ... 'International Holidays' ... Notre Dame, Indiana." This card was one on which the picture was not as crisp as it should have been. $10-15.

Rally Collector Badge [on top]. Lightweight metal with pin & clasp, 5-point 2.5" star, by WBCCI, unnumbered, dated 1974. Inscription: "WBCCI Sheriff ... Notre Dame [Indiana] ... 1974." This handsome badge has become a scarce piece of Airstream memorabilia [see also the badge accompanying the next postcard]. $25-50.

Tourist Postcard [underneath]. Used, real black & white aerial photo, 5.75" x 4", by McEwan Photo Shop, unnumbered, dated and posted 1971. Text on back of card: "Wally Byam ... Caravan Club International Inc. ... 14th International Rally ... June 28 – July 4, 1971 ... 3000 Airstream travel trailers participate at the Oregon State Fairgrounds, Salem, Marion County, Oregon." The RVers, who attended this rally and sent this postcard from Salem to friends in Norfolk, Virginia, acted as volunteers to help the rally run smoothly—according to their handwritten message on the card. They also said that they were even going to get to ride on one of the floats in the local 4th of July parade. $20-25.

Key Chain Medallion [on top]. Metal circular double-sided crest, raised graphics, 1.25" diameter, by WBCCI, unnumbered, dated 1972. Inscription: "WBCCI 15th Int'l Rally ... 1972 ... Louisville ... KY." While a handsome horse's head appeared on the front of the medallion, there was a raised design [which we have seen before] showing a tandem-axle Airstream trailer parked in a wilderness setting on the reverse side. $20-25.

Tourist Postcard [underneath]. Used, real black & white aerial photo, 5.5" x 3.5", no maker, unnumbered, dated & posted 1981. The text on the back of the card reads: "Happy Heartland Days. Iowa State Center, Ames, Iowa, site of the 24th annual Wally Byam Caravan Club International Rally. A total of 2000 trailers registered for the event held June 28th through July 4th, 1981." The US Post Office even created a special cancellation ink stamp to commemorate the rally, which read "24th Int'l Rally 81 … Ames, Iowa 50011" and which appeared on the back of this card. This postcard was sent by a couple attending the rally to friends back home in Galion, Ohio. $30-40.

Rally Collector Badge [on top]. Lightweight metal with pin & clasp, 5-point 1.75" star, by WBCCI, unnumbered, dated 1978. Inscription: "WBCCI Sheriff … Ames [Iowa] … 1978." This badge is another highly desirable Airstream collectible. $25-50.

Tourist Postcard [underneath]. Unused, real black & white aerial photo, 5.5" x 3.5", by Studio Bozeman, unnumbered, dated 1982. Reverse side text: "Silver Jubilee Roundup … 25th International Rally … June 28–July 4, 1982 … Bozeman, Montana." This 25th rally was enormous in size, as can be seen in the picture showing coaches spread over a wide area. $20-25.

Bolo Tie Medallion [on top]. Heavy metal & hard plastic circular crest, multi-color graphics, 1.75" diameter, by WBCCI, unnumbered ["Made in Korea" on back], dated 1989. Inscription: "Big Sky Celebration … Bozeman, MT … 1989." $15-20.

Advertising Postcard. Unused, real color photo, 6" x 4", no maker, unnumbered, c. 1980s-90s. Caption: "Christmas Airstream Park Inc. … Christmas All Year Round … Christmas, Florida." Interestingly, the very first words at the beginning of the text on the reverse side of this card read: "All RVs Welcome." There was undoubtedly some difficulty getting that message across when the campground's name contained the word "Airstream." $5-10.

Advertising Postcard. Used, real color photo, 6" x 4", no maker, unnumbered, posted 1992. This and the next card on this page promoted Christmas Airstream Park in Christmas, Florida. This postcard was sent from Christmas by folks staying at the park to friends in Bristol, Pennsylvania. Like the previous card, the first words printed at the top of the text on the back read: "All RVs Welcome." $5-10.

Advertising Postcard. Unused, real black & white aerial photo, 5.5" x 3.5", no maker, unnumbered, c. 1970s-80s. Travelers Rest Airstream Park in Dade City, Florida, was shown on this scarce card—with some 400 sites for Airstreams. $15-20.

Advertising Postcard. Unused, real color photo, 5.5" x 3.5", by Mitchell Color Cards, #0082-860420, 1982. Caption: "Christmas Airstream Park ... Christmas, Florida." At an earlier time, this RV camp must have been a KOA Kampground, because its A-frame office building appears to have been designed just like hundreds of classic KOA structures around the USA and Canada. $10-15.

Advertising Postcard. Unused, real color aerial photo, 5.5" x 3.5", by Frank Waley Post Cards, #1291 82, dated 1982. This card publicized the 250-site El Valle Del Sol Airstream Exclusive Trailer Park in Mission, Texas. $10-15.

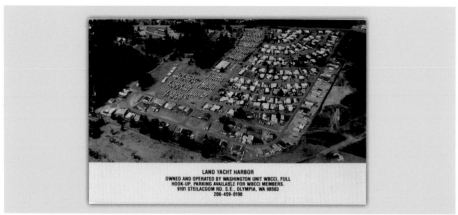

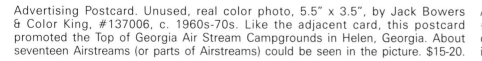

Advertising Postcard. Unused, real color aerial photo, 5.5" x 3.5", by Fitzgerald Photography & McGrew Color Graphics, #771310, c. 1970s-80s. Caption: "Land Yacht Harbor ... Owned and Operated by Washington Unit WBCCI ... Full Hook-Up, Parking Available for WBCCI Members." $10-15.

Advertising Postcard. Used, real color photo, 5.75" x 4", by House of Tyrol, #110, posted 1974. Caption: "Top of Georgia." This postcard, as with the adjacent card, publicized the Top of Georgia Airstream Trailer Park "in the beautiful North Georgia Mountains." A couple visiting this campground sent the card to friends in Scarsdale, New York, and mentioned in their handwritten message on the back—agreeing with the claim in the printed text on the back—"This is a beautiful section of Georgia." $15-20.

Advertising Postcard. Unused, real color photo, 5.5" x 3.5", by Jack Bowers & Color King, #137006, c. 1960s-70s. Like the adjacent card, this postcard promoted the Top of Georgia Air Stream Campgrounds in Helen, Georgia. About seventeen Airstreams (or parts of Airstreams) could be seen in the picture. $15-20.

Advertising Postcard. Unused, real color photo, 5.5" x 3.5", by Casa Grande Photo Shop, #111529, c. 1970s. Five Airstreams could be seen parked in the picture on this publicity card for Wheel Inn Trailer Park along route I-10 in Casa Grande, Arizona. We wanted to include this postcard as an example of several other similar cards in this book, each showing several Airstreams traveling together or parked together. Such groupings of Airstreams certainly suggest that the pictured coaches were part of a caravan or rally. $10-15.

Chapter 8

AIRSTREAM International

The early connection so firmly established by Wally Byam between Airstream trailers and international RVing has stood as one of Airstream's most creative and profound achievements in regard to both its publicity value and social significance. Byam proved to be a prophet extraordinaire in several respects over his many years at the helm at Airstream. He developed a high-profile and highly positive presence for Airstream in the foreign media and marketplace. The allure of true adventure, which Byam had instilled in his image of the Airstream, was well-suited to his extensive intercontinental caravans of Airstreams across Africa, Asia, Central America, and Europe.

Starting in the early 1950s, Wally Byam personally led a number of extended whirlwind international groups of Airstream owners and their Airstreams across many countries and to some extremely remote locations, particularly for that time in history. The media sensation caused by Byam and a large number of rugged Airstreams in a long caravan line traveling down narrow dirt and mud pathways was justifiably extraordinary. No company could have afforded the advertising and goodwill values of all of the free publicity generated by those travels.

Not surprisingly, Wally Byam and Airstream managed to incorporate plenty of references to these international escapades in their domestic US advertising (in both picture postcards and elsewhere). Airstream even sold a fair number of trailers destined to travel and reside abroad, especially in Canada and Mexico. For instance, Airstream photographer Ardean Miller actually left his Airstream trailer in Europe in storage so that he and his family could return to travel in Airstream comfort each summer for several years.

The very first international caravans ever undertaken were organized by Wally and Stella Byam and traveled to Mexico in the early 1950s.

In the summer of 1954, Wally Byam led a group on the Western Canadian Caravan, the first-ever Canadian RV caravan. Canada has been the site of two of the more than fifty annual WBCCI International Rallies. Both were held in Brandon, Manitoba, Canada, first for the 18th

AIRSTREAM LAND YACHTING—THE BETTER WAY TO TRAVEL

Advertising Postcard. Unused, real color photo, large 7" x 5.25", by Airstream, unnumbered, c. 1960. Caption: "Airstream Land Yachting—The Better Way To Travel." Truly majestic! This image is one of our favorite Airstream international photos, because it is almost unbelievable that Airstream managed to get a caravan to the pyramids in Egypt—especially to obtain permission to park the group in the wagon wheel configuration right at the base of the Great Pyramid at El Gizeh! The picture on this card was taken in 1960, and the same picture also appears on one of the postcards in the collector set released by Airstream in 2000. $40-50.

International Rally in 1975, and second for the 37th International Rally in 1994. We spend our summers each year in Downeast, Maine, so we often cross the border into Canada. We have seen many Airstreams in our travels across Canada from Newfoundland and Labrador, to Cape Breton Island and Prince Edward Island, to Alberta and British Columbia. Some of those Airstreams have belonged to other tourists like us, but many have belonged to Canadians.

We have had the opportunity to take our RV into Mexico on a number of occasions, including a fabulous and memorable trip through the Copper Canyon with the RV strapped to a flatbed railroad car. We have seen many Airstreams on those Mexican journeys—some belonging to other touristas like us, and some that were permanently stationed in Mexico.

Collector Postcard. Unused, real black & white photo, 6" x 4.25", by Airstream & Chronicle Books, unnumbered, copyright 2000. Caption: "Why not see the whole world?" This very well recognized image has appeared many times in a variety of places, and it showed an actual Airstream which, remarkably, had traveled to all of the places listed on its exterior, including numerous international locations. $5-10.

Advertising Postcard. Used, real black & white photo, large 7" x 5.25", by Airstream, unnumbered, posted 1957. Caption: "See the famous travel trailer featured in National Geographic." What a publicity coup international Airstream caravanning was! It put Airstream on center stage and way ahead of all the others in the RV industry. The back of this card, which was distributed to Airstream dealers, was printed with a rectangular area for a dealer to type or stamp its address. In turn, the dealers could send these impressive cards to prospective purchasers. This actual card was stamped by an Airstream dealer, Langhurst Motor Company of Cedar Rapids, Iowa, and sent to a possible buyer in nearby East Moline, Illinois. The picture on the card showed some of the Airstreams in the 1956 European caravan, and this photo was taken near the famous and historic Mont St. Michel along the French coastline. The text on the back touts the forty-eight-page story about "the first European trailer tour ever made" in the June 1957 issue of *NATIONAL GEOGRAPHIC* [noted and shown on page 91]. $50-75.

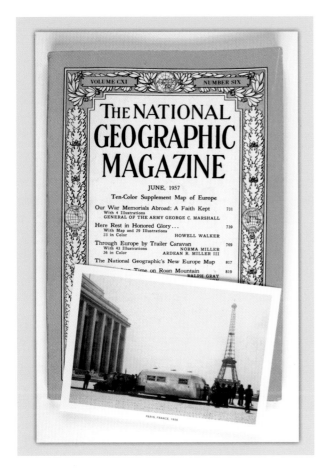

Collector Postcard. Unused, real black & white photo, 6" x 4.25", by Airstream, unnumbered, copyright 2000. Caption: "San Blas, Mexico, 1956." $5-10.

Magazine Cover & Article [underneath]. Standard magazine covers & paper, real black & white photos & color photos, 7" x 10", in *THE NATIONAL GEOGRAPHIC MAGAZINE*, "Through Europe by Trailer Caravan," by Norma Miller (with forty-three photographs by her husband Ardean Miller), forty-eight page article, June 1957. Outstanding! This scarce issue of *NATIONAL GEOGRAPHIC* is an all-time classic in the history of RVing in general, and especially in the history of Airstream. It tells the story of the 1955-56 European Airstream caravan led by Wally Byam. Norma Miller's article should be part of every RV library. For the volume, $40-50.

Collector Postcard [on top]. Unused, real black & white photo, 6" x 4.25", by Airstream, unnumbered, copyright 2000. Caption: "Paris, France, 1956." A grand image. How extraordinary it must have been to see the world's most recognized travel trailer [an Airstream] at the site of one of the world's most recognized landmarks [the Eifel Tower], particularly at that time in history! $5-10.

Collector Postcard. Unused, real black & white photo, 6" x 4.25", by Airstream, unnumbered, copyright 2000. Caption: "Barbara & Gertrude, Mexico, 1956." $5-10.

Left: Magazine Advertisement. Standard magazine paper, real black & white photos, 5.25" x 11", by Airstream, in *SUNSET*, March 1965, page 58. Caption: "Airstream puts the world at your doorstep!" This four-picture ad was used in identical versions in a number of travel and general-interest magazines. The photos showed Airstreams in a variety of international settings, including a great shot in front of the Eifel Tower in Paris. The tempting text suggested taking an Airstream to places ranging from Canada to France to the Belgian Congo. See the similar [but not identical] adjacent ad. $5-10.

Right: Magazine Advertisement. Standard magazine paper, real black & white photos, 5.25" x 11", by Airstream, in *VENTURE*, December 1964. Caption: "Adventure is calling you ... go Airstream!" Like the adjacent ad, this piece included four pictures, and it was similar in content [and identical in size]. Its text mentioned travel to Mexico, which was a nearby and, at the time, a popular country for Airstream caravans to visit. $5-10.

Advertising Postcard. Used, real color photo, 5.5" x 3.5", by Myers Studios & Dexter Color Canada, unnumbered, posted 1972. Caption: "Century Park, Morell, P.E.I." The northeastern Canadian province of Prince Edward Island is a somewhat remote, but popular, summer RV destination, as suggested by the crowd of RVs shown on this unusual three-image card. Indeed, the senders' message on the back of the postcard bemoaned the fact this campground was so full that, in order to stay in the park, they had to share "a 3-way hookup" with two other RVs. And, centered in the row of RVs in the picture was a handsome 1960s Airstream. $15-20.

Collector Postcard. Unused, real black & white photo, 6" x 4.25", by Airstream, unnumbered, copyright 2000. Caption: "Chichen Itza, Yucatan, Mexico, 1956." $5-10.

Advertising Brochures. Two, construction paper weight, real black & white photos, tri-fold design, 3.5" x 6.5" folded [10.5" x 6.5" unfolded], by Airstream, #S12, copyright 1962. Titles: *Foreign Travel with a Land Yacht*, and *The Cost of Travel with a Land Yacht*. These rare ad pieces (both stamped by the Airstream dealership named Travel Trailer Center of Franklinville and Iona, New Jersey) contained a total of seven pictures of Airstreams in various parts of the world during some of the legendary international Airstream caravan trips—in such places as El Salvador, France, Guatemala, Mexico, and South Africa. Notice that the picture on the front of the brochure on the left was the same as the picture on the postcard below. That particular brochure concluded with these inspiring words: "So plan that foreign tour. It will cost less than you think, it will be easier than you imagine, you will have more wonderful experiences than you would have believed possible." The second 1962 brochure discussing the cost of travel concluded with this remarkable comment: "We figure that ten dollars a day per couple is a little on the high side for traveling in an Airstream anywhere on earth." Each, $20-25.

Advertising Postcard. Unused, real color photo, 5.5" x 3.5", by Grant-Mann Lithographers, #S-1128, c. 1950s. The back of this card contained a space for a four cent Canadian postage stamp, and it publicized the British Columbia Forestry Camp on Okanagan Lake in Canada. An Airstream trailer was clearly visible toward the right hand side of the picture, near the end of the semi-circular row of RVs. $10-15.

Advertising Postcard. Unused, real color photo, 6" x 4", by Kap King Advertising, unnumbered, c. 1970s-80s. Klondike Valley Tent & Trailer Park in the Blackmud Creek Valley in South Edmonton, Alberta, Canada, was publicized by this unusual two-image card. An Airstream was visible near the center of the postcard. $15-20.

Advertising Postcard. Unused, real color photo, 5.5" x 3.5", by World Wide Sales Agencies, #0-12,225, c. 1960s-70s. Canada is a great place for U.S. RVers to go in the summer to escape the heat and humidity that prevails in so much of the USA. This card illustrated a busy day at Carol's Campsite in Sudbury, Ontario, Canada—with two Airstream travel trailers parked on the righthand side of the picture. $10-15.

Advertising Postcard [underneath]. Used, real color photo, 5.5" x 3.5" with scalloped edges, by PO-LO Reclame, #26630-C, posted 1968. This card, the text of which was printed partly in French and mostly in English, pictured Trailer Park Imperial & Camping near the Quebec Bridge in Quebec City, Canada. The three senders of this card were U.S. tourists who were visiting Canada, who stayed at this campground, and who sent this card to their parents in New York. Two Airstreams appeared on the right hand side of the picture—under the bridge in the background. $10-15.

Bolo Tie Medallion [on top]. Heavy metal, seven-sided crest, multi-color graphic, 1.5" diameter, by WBCCI, unnumbered, c. 1980s-90s. Inscription: "Region 2 … WBCCI." This bright and handsome medallion looked somewhat like a police badge, and it identified the seven jurisdictions included in Region 2—which was composed of both US and Canadian areas. The seven locales included Delaware, District of Columbia, Maryland, New Jersey, New York, Pennsylvania—and Ontario, Canada. WBCCI Regions 1, 2, 7, and 10 each include areas of Canada within their boundaries. $10-15.

Advertising Postcard. Used, real color photo, 5.5" x 3.5" with scalloped edges, by UNIC INC., #25868-C & #6122, c. 1960s-70s [postmark illegible, with 7 cents Canadian postage]. Youghall Trailer Park in Bathurst, New Brunswick, Canada, was the campground promoted by this card, which showed an Airstream parked just right of center in the picture. $10-15.

Publicity Postcard. Used, real black & white photo, large 7" x 5.25", by Airstream, unnumbered, dated 1959 [bulk rate postmark]. This card was sent from Jackson Center, Ohio, to an Airstream owner and/or prospective customer in East Moline, Illinois. Again, like the caravans shown in the adjacent advertisement, the group pictured here in the Costa Rica caravan was parked in the circular configuration. The text on the reverse side of the postcard promoted a television documentary *Caravan to Costa Rica (Central America)* [also described in the text as "the fabulous adventures of Wally Byam and his Airstream Caravanners"] to be aired as part of the series entitled "Bold Journey" on August 3, 1959, on ABC TV. $40-50.

Magazine Advertisement. Standard magazine paper, real black & white photo, 7" x 5", by Airstream, c. 1966. Caption: "Discover Real Travel Adventure." As the text of the ad proclaimed, Airstream was "the exciting, better way to travel anywhere in the world." Both pictures on this page illustrated Airstream international caravans parked in the famous wagon-wheel design, which Wally Byam viewed as being more democratic, for it placed everyone in an equal position and fostered attendance at group meetings, which were held in the center area of the circle. In this ad, the group of Airstreams was parked among ancient ruins and rows of ornate columns in Jerash, Jordan, in 1963. $5-10.

Advertising Postcard. Used, real black & white photo, 5.5" x 3.5", no maker, unnumbered, c. 1955 [postmark partially illegible]. This rare old publicity card for Hacienda Penuelas in Aguascalientes, Mexico, actually has some text in English on the back, as follows: "Where the Caravan of good will camped for a couple of days and, so they said, had a wonderful time." The time was so long ago that the card was addressed simply to a named person in "Slater, Mo" and, apparently, was delivered! Two Airstreams were visible at the back of the group of trailers. $30-40.

Collector Postcard. Unused, real black & white photo, 6" x 4.25", by Airstream, unnumbered, copyright 2000. Caption: "Unstoppable in Oaxaca, Mexico, 1957." $5-10.

Collector Postcard. Unused, real black & white photo, 6" x 4.25", by Airstream, unnumbered, copyright 2000. Caption: "Stella & Wally Byam, Uganda, Africa, 1960." $5-10.

Collector Postcard. Unused, real black & white photo, 6" x 4.25", by Airstream, unnumbered, copyright 2000. Caption: "Atomium, Brussels, Belgium, 1963." $5-10.

Collector Postcard. Unused, real black & white photo, 6" x 4.25", by Airstream, unnumbered, copyright 2000. Caption: "Avenue of the Sphinxes, Egypt, 1964." $5-10.

Collector Postcard. Unused, real color photo, 6" x 4.25", by Airstream, unnumbered, copyright 2000. Caption: "Bas Relief of Sapor I, Iran, 1964." $5-10.

Collector Postcard. Unused, real color photo, 6" x 4.25", by Airstream, unnumbered, copyright 2000. Caption: "Sveti Stefan, Yugoslavia, 1964." $5-10.

Top: Advertising Postcard. Unused, real color photo, smaller 5.25" x 3.25" with rounded corners, by Litho Universal & Juan Manuel, unnumbered, c. 1970s. This card and the next card both advertised the Yuca Trailer Park in Guadalajara, Jalisco, Mexico. Over the decades, since Mexico is our immediate international neighbor to the south, quite a number of Airstreams have ended up there. At least three Airstreams were visible in the photo of this small area of just one Mexican campground. $15-20.

Bottom: Advertising Postcard. Unused, real color photo, smaller 5.25" x 3.25" with rounded corners, by Litho Universal & Juan Manual, unnumbered, c. 1970s. As noted, this card also advertised the Yuca Trailer Park in Guadalajara, and again at least three more Airstream travel trailers were visible [and these trailers were not the same Airstreams shown in the other postcard photo on these pages]. $15-20.

Advertising Brochure. Standard brochure paper, real color photos, 8.5" x 11", by Airstream, 36 pages, copyright 1965. Title: *The Airstream Story*. This quite spectacular picture occupying most of page 16 of the booklet showed the curious crowd around what must have been a nearly unbelievable sight, an Airstream trailer in front of the Char Minar [which had been completed in 1591] in Hyderabad, India. For the brochure, $50-75.

Collector Postcard. Unused, real black & white photo, 4.25" x 6", by Airstream & Chronicle Books, unnumbered, copyright 2000. Caption: "Time For Tea In Holland, 1964." $5-10.

Collector Postcard. Unused, real black & white photo, 4.25" x 6", by Airstream & Chronicle Books, unnumbered, copyright 2000. Caption: "Leaning Tower of Pisa, 1964." $5-10.

Advertising Postcard. Unused, real color aerial photo, 5.5" x 7", by Buckley's Studio Ltd, #7214-D, c. 1970s. This scarce card promoted the large and popular A.E. Whidden Trailer Court in Antigonish, Nova Scotia, Canada, which is now called Whidden's Campground & Cottages. This unusual RV park has over 150 sites on some 15 acres, and it's right downtown just off Main Street. The authors have camped here a number of times over the years. Notice that at least seven Airstream trailers were parked in the long row just left of the center of the picture. $20-25.

Advertising Brochure. Standard brochure covers & paper, real color photos, 8.75" x 11", by Airstream, unnumbered, 36 pages, copyright 1965. Title: *The Airstream Story*. The cover of this brochure showed such a small section of the side of an Airstream trailer. Yet, it was instantly apparent that the image was part of an Airstream—a festive piece bearing colorful travel stickers from distant places that have been visited by Airstream caravans, like England, France, Greece, India, Italy, Russia, Spain, and Thailand. These substantial brochures containing Airstream history and product information have become highly collectible. For the brochure, $50-75.

RV Book. Cardboard covers & standard paper, real color photos, 6.75" x 8.25", *Cool Caravanning*, by Caroline Mills, 224 pages, dated 2010. Subtitle: *A Selection Of Stunning Sites In The English Countryside*. How ironic that the cover of a book about cool campsites in England would feature campers from Germany [VW Camper Vans] and from the USA [a vintage Airstream]. This nice book is a well-organized, highly informative, and handsomely done directory with some 200+ color pictures. For the book, $20-25.

Chapter 9

AIRSTREAM Look-A-Likes

With the exception of some experimentation with various styles and designs of travel trailers in its first few years in operation in the early 1930s, Airstream has quite consistently and continuously built its classic, shiny aluminum, airplane fuselage-shaped trailers. Its production for limited periods of time of Airstream motorhomes and its Argosy model trailers and its current manufacture of camper vans have been the only major departures. But, Airstream's success has generated some interesting competition. Remember that over time there have been more than 500 RV manufacturers in this country, most of which are no longer in business.

If the highest form of compliment is imitation, then Airstream is certainly a highly celebrated product. Over its 80+ years in existence, Airstream has competed with numerous look-a-likes in the travel trailer industry. Some of those competitors have produced excellent RVs, but none of them have had nearly the success of Airstream and none have remained in business.

Some of the similar looking trailers adopted aluminum exteriors or exterior colors comparable to those of Airstream. Other trailers similar in appearance to Airstream adopted some streamline design elements that Airstreams feature, such as rounded roof lines or curved front and rear sections. But alas, there is only one traditional and unique Airstream form—the classic, shiny, bullet-shape trailer. Nevertheless, without close inspection, people who are not well acquainted with Airstream may not be able to distinguish between Airstream and some of the coaches we include in the look-a-like category. Certain brands of coaches—especially Avion, Silver Streak, Spartan, and Streamline—appear almost like twins of Airstreams.

Additionally, some travel trailer brands adopted advertising and publicity methods that at times seemed quite similar in content and appearance to prior efforts of Airstream, including Airstream photographic scenes and textual slogans.

One of the travel trailer brands bearing the closest resemblance to Airstream was Silver Streak, a classy and well-built coach. Beginning

INVEST IN SILVER

Today's discriminating buyer knows a good investment when he sees one. When you invest in a Silver Streak, you move up to a travel home backed by uncompromising quality and excellence for over a quarter of a century. It's your assurance that you're making a sound investment in a future of exciting travels! We invite you to carefully examine Silver Streak travel homes. An investment in silver is a wise investment — especially if it's by Silver Streak. Write us today for the Silver Streak dealer nearest you . . . Silver Streak Trailer Company, 2319 N. Chico Ave., S. El Monte, Calif. 91733 (213) 444-2646.

TRAILER LIFE, May 1980   73

Magazine Advertisement. Standard magazine paper, real black & white photo, 4.75" x 5", by Silver Streak, in *TRAILER LIFE*, May 1980, page 73. Caption: "Invest In Silver." What a clever and apropos caption for a company named Silver Streak! Also, use of the phrase "travel home" in this ad was effective to distance the upscale Silver Streak from lesser brands of mere travel trailers and mobile homes. The picture was outstanding, leaving the impression of a superb product to rival the also superb Airstream Land Yacht. But alas, Airstream has survived; Silver Streak has not. $5-10.

in 1948-49, Silver Streak Trailer Company was located in El Monte, California, and produced trailers ranging from 19' to 31' in length. Though you don't see many Silver Streaks traveling down the highways any longer, as they were last produced in about 1997, it is not at all uncommon to find them parked permanently in campgrounds and elsewhere.

In upcoming pages, we will see several examples of both amateurish homemade coaches and professionally, factory-built trailers that incorporate some of the classic elements of the Airstream look.

Spartan was another trailer brand regularly confused with Airstream, although Spartan built only big and impressive coaches of 25 feet in length and usually longer [30-50+ feet seems to have been most common]. Spartans were built in Tulsa, Oklahoma, starting in 1946, and ending in about 1962. With rare exceptions, they are only seen parked in campgrounds, farmyards, and residential yards these days.

Perhaps the closest Airstream look-a-like was the Avion trailer, which was first manufactured in Benton Harbor, Michigan, in the mid-1950s. In the mid-1970s, Avion was bought and its traditional style trailers were produced by Fleetwood until the 1990s. Avion was roundly regarded as a good, solid coach.

Advertising Postcard. Unused, real color photo, 5.5" x 3.5", by Baxter Lane Company, #46511, date stamped 1982. This card promoted Joplin KOA Kampground in Joplin, Missouri. Over the fifty years that KOA has been in operation, numerous KOAs have produced publicity postcards that have displayed various types and brands of RVs parked at their respective campgrounds, and Airstreams have been popular fixtures in quite a number of those postcard pictures. But here, a Silver Streak [toting its recognizable rear storage locker] had arrived at the camp office. From the front and sides, Silver Streak trailers looked far more like Airstreams than they did from the rear (particularly, if they were fitted with the storage box). $15-20.

Advertising Postcard. Unused, real color photo, 5.5" x 3.5", by Living Colour Advertising & Dexter Press, #87600-B, c. 1960s. Here, the Mountain View Auto Court and Trailer Park in Vancouver, British Columbia, Canada, was shown with a long and handsome Silver Streak trailer parked near the highway. According to the text on the back of the card, Mountain View was "A Home Away From Home." At a glance, many people would think the pictured coach was an Airstream. $10-15.

Magazine Advertisement. Standard magazine paper, real black & white photo, 7.5" x 5.5", by Silver Streak, in *TRAIL-R-NEWS MAGAZINE*, March 1958, page 92. Caption: "Silver Streak … One of the Finest Travel Trailers Built …" Notice the emphasis (much like some promotional statements of Airstream) on "all metal riveted aircraft type construction." Interestingly, this ad called Silver Streak "one of the finest" coaches, but before long, as you will see in the other pieces illustrated on these pages, Silver Streak began to call its coaches "the finest" RVs built. Part of the reason for the early and temporary success of Silver Streak was the similarity of appearance and quality to Airstream. $5-10.

Rubber RV Toy. Thick soft rubber, restored truck & 5th wheel toy with six tires, 5" x 1.5" x 1.5", by Sun Rubber Company, #1020, c. 1930s. This toy is a well-known early RV toy, made by a prominent toy maker of the era. It is a truck with a 5th wheel travel trailer attached (in real life the two parts could be unhitched and separated, although the two pieces of the toy were permanently joined). The toy looked much like the vehicles that appear in the print ads on this page. This particular toy has been restored at some point in its life—the wheels have been replaced and it has been repainted an Airstream-style silver color. $25-50.

Advertising Postcard. Used, real color photo, 5.5" x 3.5", by Quality Postcards, unnumbered, copyright 1987 [posted 1992]. Caption: "Silver Streak … The Finest Travel Trailer Built." Notice that this trailer even sported curved aluminum roof panels, similar to those of older Airstreams. A lot of people have mistaken Silver Streak trailers for Airstreams. This postcard is a well-known one. $10-15.

RV Toy. Japanese tin toy travel trailer with rolling wheels and working side entry door, by Bandai brand, 8.5" x 3.5" x 4", c. 1980s. Japanese toy manufacturers have made many RV toys in the post-WWII decades, including several trailers that look much like Airstreams. This mint-condition toy appears to be somewhat of a cross between an Airstream [with the silver-gray aluminum exterior and eleven curved front and rear roof panels] and a Silver Streak [also with the aluminum finish, but with the more boxy rounded roof shape]. This trailer is part of a two-piece set that also includes a friction-powered dune buggy style tow car. For the trailer toy, $30-40.

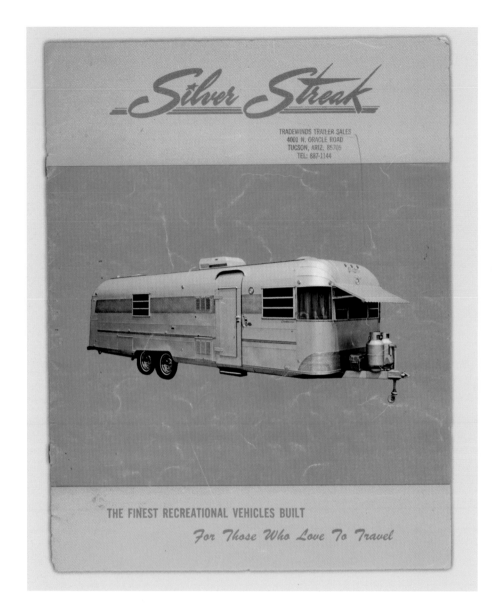

Advertising Postcard. Used, real color photo, 5.5" x 3.5", Schaaf Post Card Company, unnumbered, copyright 1976 [posted 1980]. This card promoted Martins Trailer Park in Deming, New Mexico, where the family of four senders of this postcard were staying. Apparently new to RVing, their message on the back commented: "Trailer life is certainly different." If you look closely, you see both a Silver Streak [with its distinctive rear storage box] to the left side of the picture and an Airstream parked next to it on the right. What a coincidence. $10-15.

Advertising Brochure. Heavy brochure paper, real color photos, 8.5" x 11", by Silver Streak, unnumbered, 8 pages, c. 1970s. Title: *Silver Streak*, with the name and contact information of a local dealership stamped on the front [Tradewinds Trailer Sales in Tucson, Arizona]. At the time this brochure was printed, Silver Streak had been in business "for the past 20 odd years," and the company emphasized that it produced "the ultimate in aircraft-type constructed" RVs—as did Airstream boast of its airplane fuselage design. Many of the Silver Streak models were embellished with the gold accents shown on the coach on the cover of this brochure, and the distinctive gold features helped promote Silver Streak's quality claim: "The Finest Recreational Vehicles Built." As we noted earlier, the company had moved from calling its coach "one of the finest" to "the finest." $25-50.

Advertising Postcard. Used, real color photo, 5.5" x 3.5", by Atlantic Publishing & Dexter Press, #79840-C, posted 1973. Caption/Sign: "Apache Camp Ground." The text on the back of this five-picture card publicized Apache Family Campground in Myrtle Beach, South Carolina, a huge ocean-front park with more than 1000 sites. The senders of the postcard in their handwritten message said this campground was "very nice." The card was sent up the coast to a couple in Laurel, Maryland. An Airstream can be seen in the lower left photo, and either a Silver Streak or Streamline trailer was shown in the upper left photo. $10-15.

Old Amateur Photographs [3 photos – upper left & bottom row]. Vintage photograph paper, real black & white photos, 5" x 3.5" with scalloped edges, unknown photographer, unnumbered [#803A on back of each picture apparently is photo lab number], c. 1940s-50s. These three family photos illustrate what may have been a little homemade travel trailer only about 10-15 feet long, although there were so many small trailer makers in those early days that it might have been commercially produced. Again, like Airstream, this trailer was cleverly different—aluminum, aerodynamic, lightweight, creative, and uniquely shaped. We wonder if the young boy in the photo (like the young Wally Byam) grew up to be an RV manufacturing executive? For the group, $20-25.

Comic Postcard [upper right]. Unused, multi-color linen, 5.5" x 3.5", by Curt Teich & Co., #C-277 & #7A-H2467, c. 1930s-40s. Caption: "O Carefree days of vagabond bliss! Be it ever so humble, home was never like this!" This rare card has a box on the back to "place [a] one cent stamp here," and the card was part of the "C. T. Everyday Comics" series. Notice how the small, aluminum trailer on this comedy postcard looks just like the little trailer in the adjacent family photos. $30-40.

Tourist Postcard. Unused, real black & white photo, 5.5" x 3.5", by Judd & Detweiler, unnumbered, c. 1940s-50s. Caption: "NCCS Bookmobile." The text on the back of this rare card said: "This Bookmobile, operated by National Catholic Community Service, member agency of USO, is bringing literature, writing materials, stamps, and making other facilities available to service men on maneuvers." Look at the close similarities between the trailer pictured here and the one on the adjacent postcard. What features do these trailers share with Airstreams? The metal construction, rounded roof lines, and silver-gray color would cause some people to think Airstream. $25-50.

Tourist Postcard. Unused, real black & white photo, 5.5" x 3.5", by American Lutheran Publicity Bureau & Eagle Post Card View Company, unnumbered, c. 1940s-50s. Caption: "The Trailer Chapel at Franklin, New Hampshire." The text on the back of this scarce card reads: "The Trailer Chapel is a church on wheels sponsored by the church of the Lutheran Hour. It operates in the towns and cities of Northern New England." The trailer has some characteristics similar to those of Airstreams (like the trailer on the adjacent card—metal construction, silver-gray color, and somewhat curved-aerodynamic design), so some people would confuse them. $25-50.

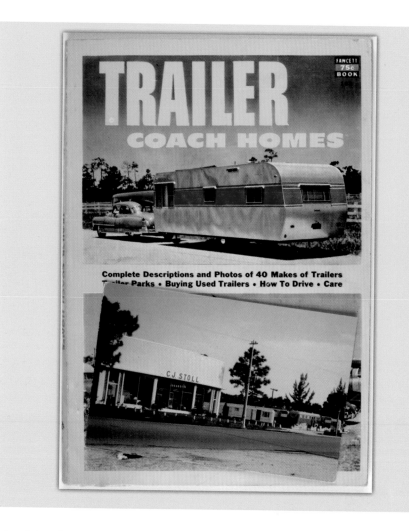

Advertising Catalogue [underneath]. Heavy magazine-grade cover & standard paper, real color photos on cover with black & white photos inside, 6.5" x 9.5", by Fawcett Book, #163, 146 pages, copyright 1952. Entitled: *Trailer Coach Homes*. This image appeared on the upper portion of the front cover of the booklet. The booklet is now a marvelous piece of RV history, recording hundreds of pictures and details about forty brands of travel trailers and mobile homes, several of which have likenesses somewhat similar to Airstreams—including Alma, Silverdome, Zimmer, and the shiny aluminum coach pictured on the cover of the publication. For the catalogue, $50-75.

Advertising Postcard [on top]. Unused, real color photo, 5.5" x 3.5", by C. J. O'Brien & Dexter Press, #62009, c. 1950s. Caption: "C. J. Stoll." C. J. Stoll Trailer Sales of both Tampa and St. Petersburg, Florida was the company advertised on this card, the text of which claimed the dealership had the "World's Largest Indoor Trailer Sales." Further, the text on the back of this postcard pointed out Stoll was a distributor for Lutes, Schult, Travelo, and Vagabond brand travel trailers. Notice that the trailer in the center of the picture is a metal, silver-gray coach with rounded and somewhat streamlined rooflines—as was Airstream. $15-20.

Magazine Advertisement [underneath]. Standard magazine paper, real black & white photo, 5.5" x 8.5", by Trailer Coach Manufacturers Association, dated 1948. Caption: "See More ... Stay Longer." That slogan sounds rather similar to the Airstream motto: "See More ... Do More ... Live More." Hence, the similarities between Airstream and other travel trailers can take a number of forms. This magazine ad listed forty specific, named trailer companies, from Adams to Zimmer and including such well-known brands as National, Palace, Prairie-Schooner, Schult, Travelo, Trotwood, and Vagabond. Yet, while Airstream has thrived over the last eighty plus years, not one of those other forty trailer companies has survived. $10-15.

Vintage Photograph [on top]. Vintage black & white photo paper, small 2.75" x 3.75" with art-deco graphic border, #69 [apparently the photo lab processing number], dated 1936. Wow, another rare find! This wonderful and unique, very old picture shows a lady with her dog and presumably their trailer—which has both the basic shape and exterior finish appearance of an Airstream. But, it's not an Airstream. The handwritten note on the back of the picture identified the date and location as February of 1936 in Punta Gorda, Florida. $20-25.

Business Appointment Postcard. Unused, real color photo, 6" x 4", no maker [British], unnumbered, c. 1960s. Caption [in the photo]: "Bayly Bartlett Ltd ... Mobile Showroom." The reverse side of this scarce appointment card was pre-printed as an invitation to visit the English company's Mobile Showroom—with blank spaces to be filled in for the location, date, and time. The business is no longer in operation. $30-40.

Italian Tourist Postcard. Used, real color photo, 5.75" x 3", by Innocenti, #24, c. 1960s-70s [postmark illegible]. Remarkable find! This oddly-sized card showcased the Michelangelo Esplanade in Florence, Italy, and its picture included a small, silver-gray bullet-shaped travel trailer that looks a lot like an Airstream. The postcard was mailed from Florence, Italy, to someone in Baddeck, Nova Scotia, Canada [where we acquired the card while on an RV trip]. $20-25.

Portugal Tourist Postcard. Used, real color photo, 5.75" x 4", no maker, unnumbered, dated 1969 [written but not posted]. This picturesque card advertised the campground Camping Monsanto in Lisbon, Portugal. Pictured in the middle in the foreground of the postcard was a small, silver, metal, streamlined travel trailer—reminiscent of an Airstream. $15-20.

Tourist Postcard. Unused, real color photo, 5.5" x 3.5", by Pensacola News Agency & Curteichcolor, #6C-K1530, c. 1950s. The text on the back of the card reads: "Fabulous Palafox Street ... Pensacola, Florida." Centered in the foreground of this rare card was a silver-gray, metal travel trailer with curved front and rear rooflines. $20-25.

Advertising Postcard. Unused, real color photo, 5.5" x 3.5", by Dexter Press & M. C. Kalfus, #91566-B, c. 1960s. This vintage card publicized Myers Motel & Edge O Town Trailer Court in Klamath, California, and carried a very simple message on the back: "A nice place to stay." Like the other travel trailers highlighted on these pages, the little silver trailer in the foreground of the picture would have looked like an Airstream to many people because of its small size, aluminum appearance, and curved shape. $15-20.

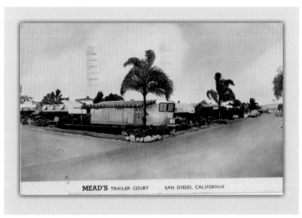

Advertising Postcard. Used, chrome, 5.5" x 3.5", by E. B. Thomas, #E-12099, posted 1952. Caption: "Mead's Trailer Court ... San Diego, California." The travel trailer featured in the center of this card was a classic Spartan coach, probably 25-30 feet in length. It had a shiny aluminum exterior and a somewhat streamline design—so it looked a lot like an Airstream to many people. The senders of this postcard were in the midst of an extended stay at Mead's RV park. $20-25.

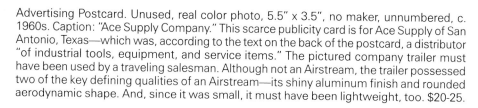

Advertising Postcard. Unused, real color photo, 5.5" x 3.5", no maker, unnumbered, c. 1960s. Caption: "Ace Supply Company." This scarce publicity card is for Ace Supply of San Antonio, Texas—which was, according to the text on the back of the postcard, a distributor "of industrial tools, equipment, and service items." The pictured company trailer must have been used by a traveling salesman. Although not an Airstream, the trailer possessed two of the key defining qualities of an Airstream—its shiny aluminum finish and rounded aerodynamic shape. And, since it was small, it must have been lightweight, too. $20-25.

Advertising Postcard. Unused [sample card], linen, 5.5" x 3.5", by E. C. Kropp & R. C. Shaul, #29210N, dated 1951. Caption: "Bradbury Trailer Sales ... U.S. Hwy. 1, West Peabody, Mass." This particular card served as the sales sample for the postcard for Bradbury Trailers, which sold Spartan RVs. Like Airstream's design based upon the airplane fuselage shape, the text on the back of the card refers to Bradbury as "Dealers in Spartan Aircraft Coaches." Spartan produced a handsome, good quality coach, but—unlike Airstream—Spartan did not survive. $20-25.

Advertising Postcard. Unused, real color photo, 6" x 4", by Gibbs Smith, Publisher, unnumbered, c. 2005. Caption: "Douglas Keister ... *Silver Palaces*." This publicity card for Doug Keister's then-new book, entitled *Silver Palaces: America's Streamlined Trailers*, showed a handsome vintage Spartan coach—which again had attributes known especially to Airstreams, such as its small size, aluminum exterior, and streamline design. Keister, who we know as a friend and colleague in the publishing field, is a prolific author and "vintage trailer expert," whose outstanding books include several on RVing, not surprisingly with a number focusing considerable attention on Airstreams [see our Bibliography for a list of his impressive RV works, and see keisterphoto.com]. $10-15.

Magazine Advertisement. Standard magazine paper, real black & white photo, 7.5" x 5", by Streamline Trailer Company, in *TRAIL-R-NEWS MAGAZINE*, March 1958, page 96. Caption: "Streamline Trailer Co. ... Personalized luxury travel trailers." The pictured coach was quite attractive and appeared so similar to an Airstream. The Streamline ad referred to its "aircraft construction" and its "aluminum" exterior, like Airstream. As with so many trailer brands, Streamline did not survive, even though it boasted of building "personalized luxury travel trailers" which were "engineered and designed as a result of [a] survey of actual users [of] this type trailer." $5-10.

Magazine Advertisement [right]. Standard magazine paper, real black & white photo, small 2.25" x 3.25", by Avion, dated 1961. Caption: "Go for game in an Avion travel trailer." This ad and the adjacent postcard showed hunters using Avion coaches, which purpose to this day remains one of the popular uses of RVs. In fact, all kinds of sporting people utilize RVs as their base camps in both remote areas and populated places. Avion looked like it could be the twin to Airstream. $5-10.

Advertising Postcard [left]. Unused, real color photo, 5.5" x 3.5", by Tichnor Brothers, #K-12653, c. 1960s. This card promoted Avion trailers, and the slogan printed in the text on the back of the postcard read: "World's finest travel trailers." The card showed an Avion coach and two outdoorsmen hunting with their dog out in the woods. It was an effective setting for a travel trailer advertisement. $20-25.

Magazine Advertisement [left]. Standard magazine paper, real black & white photo, small 2.5" x 4", by Avion, c. 1960s. Caption: "Discover Avion Trailer traveling … for more fun, comfort, savings." The handsome picture showed a sophisticated tow car and Avion coach pairing in front of the famous Mexico City Cathedral. Airstream attained highly successful publicity from its numerous international caravan expeditions beginning in the 1950s, and some of Airstream's competitors (especially with their look-a-like trailers) felt the need also to project a foreign presence. Indeed, the content of this Avion ad sounded much like earlier Airstream advertisements. This Avion piece even adopted a phrase ["see more, do more, and save more"] which was awfully similar to the well-known Airstream slogan ["See more … Do more … Live more"]. $5-10.

Advertising Postcard [right]. Unused, real color photo, 5.5" x 3.5", by Freeman Studios, #60439, c. 1960s. This card illustrated the 27' Avion Travelcader, and on the back of the card its text reads: "Far-off places seem suddenly closer in this veteran mile-maker." The "far-off" place that was the setting for this postcard picture could have been Holland, with the tulips in the foreground and the old-fashioned windmill in the background—but, it was undoubtedly somewhere right here in the US. Doesn't this postcard remind you of so many Airstream publicity shots actually taken in various well-known locations around the globe? $20-25.

Advertising Postcard. Unused, real color photo, 5.5" x 3.5", by Brunson Sales Company, #46973, c. 1950s. This publicity card for Paradise Palms Trailer Park in Mesa, Arizona, focused attention on the campground swimming pool, which had a long, shiny, aluminum Spartan trailer as the backdrop next to the pool. $10-15.

Advertising Postcard. Used, real color photo, 5.5" x 3.5", by Freeman Studios, #67165, posted 1964. This scarce publicity card illustrated the 18' Avion Sportsman model trailer that looked so much like an Airstream. Curiously, the text on the back of the postcard referenced the trailer's "lifetime guarantee"—although the company went out of business, leaving many living Avion owners without the promised warranty. The card was sent intrastate from San Marcos to Long Beach, California. $20-25.

Advertising Postcard. Unused, real color photo, 5.5" x 3.5", by Freeman Studios, #60440, c. 1960s. This card showed the 24' Avion Holiday model trailer, describing it as a "hardy" coach with a "zestful flair for traveling." In the end, the impressive Avion trailer simply could not continue to compete with Airstream. $20-25.

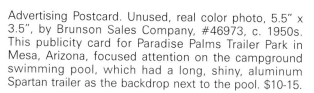

Advertising Postcard. Unused, real color photo, 5.5" x 3.5", by Chevrolet, unnumbered, dated 1991. Caption: "91 ... Suburban." This automobile advertising card promoted the 1991 Chevy Suburban, towing a handsome Avion travel trailer—in virtually the same staged pose as Airstream trailers occupied many times behind numerous and different makes and models of cars and trucks. $5-10.

Advertising Postcard. Used, real color photo, 5.5" x 3.5", by Avion, unnumbered, posted 1962. Text on the back of this card: "Avion Travel Trailers & Pickup Campers ... The great-idea recreational vehicles for the ultimate in travel luxury." Didn't the trailer pictured here look like the twin, or at least the close kin, of an Airstream? Avion also produced camper sections for pick-up trucks, as shown here. $15-20.

Advertising Postcard. Unused, real color photo, 5.5" x 3.5", by Cline Advertising & Color King, #126904, c. 1960s. This card publicized Dudley Creek Travel Trailer Park "In The Great Smokies" in Gatlinburg, Tennessee, which the text on the back of the postcard announced is "ideally located to park your 'home-away-from-home'." Wouldn't you have to look closely to determine that the trailer in the foreground of the picture was an Avion, rather than an Airstream? $10-15.

RV Tourist Postcard. Used [but not mailed], real black & white photo, 5.5" x 3.25", by Photo-Graphics, unnumbered, dated 1970. Caption: "Avion International Travelcade Club Summer Rendezvous ... Coldwater, Michigan ... July 1970." Just as Airstream did so successfully with its various local, regional, and national rallies and its national and international caravans, other trailer manufacturers also sponsored similar gatherings. This scarce card's aerial picture showed the sizable 1970 Avion Summer Rendezvous, and the handwritten note on the back of the postcard says that the hand-noted "x" on its front marked the spot where the writers stayed at the rally. Their note also reported that 818 trailers were in attendance at one point during the rally. $20-25.

Advertising Postcard. Unused, real color photo, 5.5" x 3.5", by The Whites, #14160, c. 1960s-70s. What a challenge to identify these RVs! Maybe this group was attending a rally. There are seven similar trailers lined up the slope in this picture, all looking like Airstreams. They were parked at North Fork Campsites along the Shenandoah River in Front Royal, Virginia (which is advertised by the postcard). But, none of the coaches appear to really be Airstreams. Instead, they are Avions. $30-40.

Magazine Advertisement. Standard magazine paper, real black & white and color photos, large 10.5" x 13.75", by International Harvester Company, in *COLLIER'S*, June 29, 1940, page 23. Caption: "Commander Gatti Returns from Belgian Congo with Great Enthusiasm for International Trucks." Fantastic find! This colorful and historic ad commemorated the return of African explorer Attilio Gatti with his two luxurious and futuristic International Harvester "Jungle Yacht" pairs of trucks and 5th wheel travel trailers. They were of metal construction, streamlined design, and silver-gray exterior finish. And, they were "Yachts!" Sound familiar? $30-40.

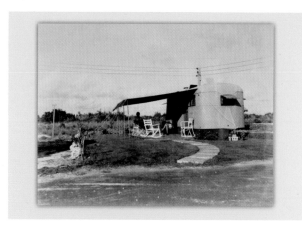

Tourist Postcard. Used, real black & white photo, 5.25" x 3.5", no maker, unnumbered, posted 1953. This card was sent from South Dakota to Nebraska. The RV pictured here was a Spartan, about 25-30 feet long. The sender's message on the back of the rare card actually said: "This is our new house." Maybe it was? $25-50.

Classified Advertisement. Standard magazine paper, real black & white photos, small 5" x 3", c. 1940s. Caption: "'Continental Clipper'—Custom-Built Land Yacht—For Sale." The ad called this coach "America's most luxurious trailer." It was built in 1938 for an original price of $35,000. This ad offered both the 1.5 ton truck and 5th wheel trailer for $12,750. It had a number of owners prior to this time—including King Farouk of Egypt, a Maharaja in India, and a New York businessman. $10-15.

Vintage Photograph. Standard vintage photo paper, real black & white photo, 5.25" x 4", #005 [probably the processing lab number], c. late 1940s-50s. This wonderful old trailer possessed some of the features of Airstream, with its silver-gray color, its metal exterior, and its streamline accents (the rounded roofline and v-shaped extension over the A-frame tow coupler). Of course, it was not Airstream. $20-25.

Advertising Postcard. Unused, real color photo, 5.5" x 3.5", by McCoy Color Studio & Dexter Press, #62148-B, c. 1960s. The text on the back of the card said simply: "Silver Streak … El Monte, California … The Finest Travel Trailer Built." In order to help promote the upscale image of Silver Streak, the trailer on this card was being towed by a Cadillac, with its large and streamlined tail fins. To the casual observer, this trailer looked just like an Airstream. $10-15.

Advertising Postcard. Used, real color photo, 5.5" x 3.5", by Colourpicture, #P55351, posted 1964. This scarce publicity card showed the long 31' Streamline Count, and the postcard was sent from the company's office in Thorntown, Indiana, to a prospective customer in Washington, D.C. Streamline also had an office in El Monte, California. Doesn't it seem, with so many elements in common, that this impressive, upscale coach would have been associated with Airstream? $20-25.

Advertising Postcard. Unused, real color photo, 5.5" x 3.5" with rounded corners, by Ross Hall Studio & Dexter Press, #E-40788, c. 1950s. Chris and May's Pend Oreille Lake Resort on Lake Pend Oreille in Hope, Idaho, was the campground publicized by this old card. Near the center of the picture was an Airstream-looking coach, which in reality appears to be either a Silver Streak or Streamline trailer. $20-25.

Chapter 10

AIRSTREAM Art & Humor

From the very beginning of Airstream, it was clear that Wally Byam and others in authority were creative and thoughtful, and were possessed of good senses of style and humor. These progressive characteristics permeated everything about Airstream, from the design features of its trailers, to the development of its unique fringe benefits for Airstream owners [including international caravans, and Airstream exclusive parks and rallies], to its unmatched advertising campaigns.

In a sense, this chapter might be considered redundant, for so many of the pieces included already have displayed fine graphic and scenic artistry, as well as instances of lighthearted and humorous moments. Particularly striking have been the numerous examples of the memorable photographs taken by Airstream's masterful photographer Ardean Miller.

It has been observed many times that the classic Airstream trailer is a genuine work of modern art. Born during the art deco era, this conclusion about the artistic merit of Airstream trailers should come as no surprise. Airstreams are bright and shiny; Airstreams are streamlined and stylish; Airstreams are cultural icons as much as they are commercial legends; and, Airstreams are unique and are here to stay. An Airstream is a trophy for its owners, as bright and unmistakable as an Oscar or an Emmy, and deserving to be cherished and preserved. In a fascinating article entitled "The Art Of Airstream," Forrest McClure in the Summer 2009 issue of *AIRSTREAM LIFE* reviewed recent instances in which individuals and institutions have acknowledged the artistic merits of Airstreams, and concluded with this comment about Airstream: "It is an icon, and now not just the subject of artistic expression, but art itself."

The wonderfully realistic images appearing on these pages are the works of artist Paige Bridges, who paints Airstreams with a passion that is apparent. Her original paintings, prints, and postcards of Airstreams and other RVs can be seen and purchased at VintageTravelTrailerArt.com.

Tourist Postcard. Unused, multi-color graphic, 6" x 4", by *AIRSTREAM LIFE*, unnumbered, c. 2000s. Caption: "Rest Stop." This handsome card is, of course, a clever, but simple, variation on the original and famous 1942 oil painting of a late-night view of a New York City diner entitled *Night Hawks* by renowned artist Edward Hopper. Here, an Airstream has been added. The reverse side of the postcard is pre-printed for use as a tourist card with text and blank spaces for the sender to complete. The card can be purchased in quantities at airstreamlife.com/store. $5-10.

We sincerely appreciate our friend Paige Bridges' assistance in gathering together this group of outstanding examples of her Airstream art. We want her to keep painting Airstreams!

The happy and whimsical Airstream scenes shown are watercolor illustrations done by British artist Annabel Tarrant, whose works are regularly available for purchase on eBay and at annabel.tarrant@btinternet.com. She is a devoted Airstream owner who delights in traveling in her 1967 Caravel. We extend our sincere thanks to our friend Annabel for her help in presenting this group of fun images. We hope to see more Airstream illustrations from her!

We thank our friend and artist Bob Meredith for his cooperation in showing his outstanding prints. His RV pieces can be found at TinCanTourists.com. We want him to keep on painting!

Artist Mary Sundstrom's affinity for Airstreams and her fine talent in painting them earned her a feature article entitled "Airstream Artist Mary Sundstrom" in the Winter 2007 issue of *AIRSTREAM LIFE* magazine. Her marvelous work can be found on her website at www.airstreamart.com. We thank our friend Mary for her assistance in showing these pieces in this book. We hope she will keep painting her fun Airstreams!

Art Postcard. Unused, reproduction of original casein painting, large 8.5" x 5.5", by artist Paige Bridges, unnumbered, copyright 2005. Entitled: *Heaven On Earth*. Heaven in this case is a scene with four Airstreams and two pink flamingos. $5-10.

Art Postcard. Unused, reproduction of original casein painting, large 8.5" x 5.5", by artist Paige Bridges, unnumbered, copyright 2010. Entitled: *Airlight At Yellowstone*. The trailer in this painting is not an Airstream, but many people would assume it's an Airstream. This wonderful painting illustrates a rare rear-entry 1955 Airlight travel trailer, being towed through Yellowstone National Park by a 1950s era Studebaker pick-up truck. $5-10.

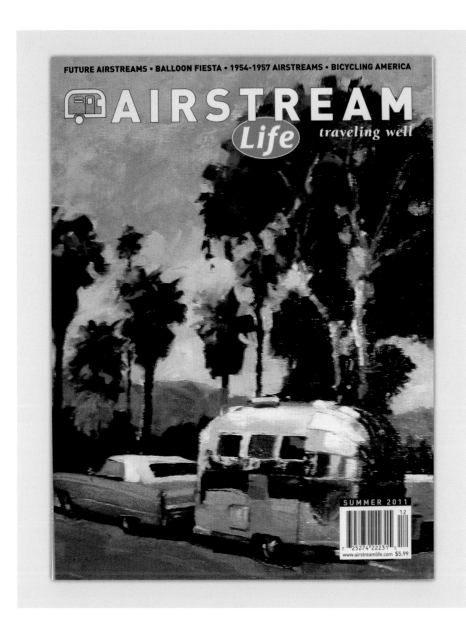

Magazine Cover. Standard magazine cover, reproduction of an oil painting, 8" x 11", in *AIRSTREAM LIFE*, by professional artist and commercial illustrator Bob Brugger, Summer 2011. Here is a perfect, classic RV pair—a Cadillac and an Airstream. For the full issue, $10-15.

Art Postcard. Unused, reproduction of original watercolor painting, 5.5" x 4.25", by artist Mary Sundstrom, unnumbered, 2004. Title: *Airstream Night Glow*. This picture by Mary Sundstrom is just one of several fun and clever Airstream pieces that she has painted, and that can be found at www.airstreamart.com. At the end of this chapter are two more examples of her prints showing Mary's wonderful creativity and skill with Airstreams as her subject. For the postcard, $5-10.

Art Postcard. Unused, reproduction of original casein painting, large 8.5" x 5.5", by artist Paige Bridges, unnumbered, copyright 2009. Entitled: *Gettin' Ready*. This picture is one of the few done by Paige Bridges in which a person is present in the work. Shown here are a 1953 Chevy truck and a 1968 Airstream Land Yacht. $5-10.

Art Postcard. Unused, reproduction of original casein painting, 5.5" x 4.25", by artist Paige Bridges, unnumbered, copyright 2003. Entitled: *Flower Child*. The trailer in this picture is an Airstream Cruisette, not a Bambi as some might think, and it's the "Flower Child." The symmetry is fun—with the beach blanket and chairs to one side, the VW in the middle, and the American flag on the other side. $5-10.

Art Postcard. Unused, reproduction of original casein painting, large 8.5" x 5.5", by artist Paige Bridges, unnumbered, copyright 2008. Entitled: *Safe Haven*. This serene work was commissioned by the owner of the featured 1965 Airstream Globe Trotter. $5-10.

Holiday Art Postcard. Unused, reproduction of original casein painting, large 8.5" x 5.5", by artist Paige Bridges, unnumbered, copyright 2007. Entitled: *Home For Christmas*. If we dare to dream of a snowy Christmas, all of us who own Airstreams would love this picture to be our holiday home. $5-10.

Holiday Art Postcard. Unused, reproduction of original casein painting, large 8.5" x 5.5", by artist Paige Bridges, unnumbered, c. 2000s. Entitled: *Silent Night*. The setting for this picture of a 1968 Airstream Caravel is Glacier National Park. $5-10.

Holiday Art Postcard. Unused, reproduction of original casein painting, large 8.5" x 5.5", by artist Paige Bridges, unnumbered, copyright 2008. Entitled: *O Christmas Tree*. The vintage Airstream pictured here has the classic thirteen roof panels. $5-10.

Holiday Art Postcard. Unused, reproduction of original casein painting, large 8.5" x 5.5", by artist Paige Bridges, unnumbered, copyright 2007. Entitled: *Christmas Camping*. Among the seven vintage trailers in this scene, how many can you identify? There is a Shasta, a Spartan, and, of course, an Airstream. What else? $5-10.

Holiday Art Postcard. Unused, reproduction of original casein painting, large 8.5" x 5.5", by artist Paige Bridges, unnumbered, copyright 2003. Entitled: *Vintage Christmas*. The warmth in this image is produced in large part by the golden glow coming from inside the old Airstream. $5-10.

Holiday Art Postcard. Unused, reproduction of original casein painting, large 8.5" x 5.5", by artist Paige Bridges, unnumbered, c. 2000s. Entitled: *Vintage Tree Lot*. A perfectly-kept vintage Airstream trailer makes a fantastic and upscale sales office for a Christmas tree lot! $5-10.

Brochure Cover [underneath]. Heavy brochure cover paper, real black & white [colored] photo, 11" x 8.5", by Airstream, 30 pages, copyright 2007. Title: *Airstream ... See More ... Do More ... Live More*. This 1947 publicity stunt and picture may be the most recognized of all Airstream images. Airstream has used this photograph many times over the years—for a very sound reason. It's truly special. The publicity photo showed Airstream was a lightweight trailer that could be towed by a bicyclist. Also, this particular contemporary brochure was special because it was so detailed, with sections telling about Airstream history and design, including a two-page graphic of the entire product-line history of nearly eighty years, and showing the current models of Airstreams, with some forty excellent photographs. For the brochure, $20-25.

Collector Postcard [on top]. Unused, multi-color graphics, reproduction of 1950s Airstream 33" x 26" poster, 6" x 4.25", by Country Music Foundation & Chronicle Books, unnumbered, copyright 2001. This simple and sophisticated illustration of an Airstream trailer was taken from the Hatch Show Prints: 40 Collectible Postcards published by Chronicle Books. The very scarce and genuinely stunning postcard has become a highly sought Airstream piece. $20-25.

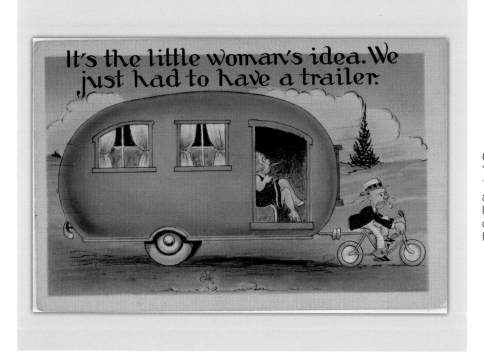

Comic Postcard. Used, linen, 5.5" x 3.5", no maker, #1485, posted 1939. Caption: "It's the little woman's idea. We just had to have a trailer." A most clever card for its 1930s vintage. This fun postcard shows a dapper fellow (wearing a sport coat, tie, and matching hat) riding a very small bicycle and towing a bright orange [pumpkin-like] travel trailer with the "little woman" (who looks larger than him, who is also well-dressed and who is smoking a cigarette) riding inside the trailer. Remarkably, as we have seen, in 1947 Airstream actually got a bicyclist to pull one of its coaches. $15-20.

Advertising Postcard. Unused, real color photo, 5.5" x 3.5", by R. E. Whitmore, unnumbered, c. 1970s. Caption: "It only takes one horsepower to pull a Shasta." This particular card became a very well-known and effective Shasta publicity card, showing a trailer bearing the classic "wings-of-Shasta" emblem on the upper rear section of the side of the coach. The text on the back of the postcard proclaimed Shasta is "America's No 1 selling travel trailer." If Airstream could be towed by a single bicyclist, did this card represent Shasta's response—that it too could easily be towed, in this instance by a single horse which was also pulling an Amish wagon? $10-15.

Collector Postcard. Unused, real black & white photo, 6" x 4.25", by Airstream & Chronicle Books, unnumbered, copyright 2000. Caption: "French Bicycle Racer Latourneau Pulls An Airstream, 1947." This card represents one more use of this iconic image. Do you think Wally Byam and the other people in charge at Airstream in 1947 could have really imagined how widespread this one picture would come to be used? It's as much a company symbol as the Airstream name. $5-10.

Magazine Advertisement [underneath]. Standard magazine paper, real black & white photo, full-page 8" x 11", by Airstream, in *TRAIL-R-NEWS*, March 1958, page 14. Caption: "Proven By Ponderous Pachyderm! ... Airstream combines fantastic strength with unmatched lightness." This advertising stunt showed Big Babe, a 9700 pound circus elephant standing on an Airstream chassis. The text of the ad went on to point out "the elephant is considered to be the most intelligent of all large animals ... and an elephant will positively not set foot on any surface that is not absolutely firm and unyielding. Yet, this five-ton behemoth willingly stepped aboard the Airstream chassis and walked around." $5-10.

Advertising Postcard [on top]. Used, real color photo, cardboard coaster-weight stock, 5" x 3.5" with rounded corners, by Craig DeMartino & New Belgium Brewing, unnumbered, posted 2005. Caption: "Beerstream Dream Team ... New Belgium ... Fort Collins, Colorado USA." What a unique and fun card! It's a beer ad on a coaster that doubles as a postcard. The text on the reverse side states: "Team Beerstream and their 1967 Airstream Safari dutifully patrol the New Belgium territories, educating palates and delighting minds. Watch for their next shining appearance in your town." The clever picture appears staged so as to make it look like the Airstream is being pulled by the Dream Team bicyclists. $20-25.

Holiday Art Card. Standard glossy card stock, bi-fold greeting card, reproduction of watercolor illustration, 7.25" x 4.5" folded [7.25" x 9" unfolded], by British artist Annabel Tarrant, unnumbered, 2010. Entitled: *Snowstream*. Printed greeting inside card: "happy holidays" [with prints of two dog paws]. On this clever card, the snow has covered both the flamingos in the yard and the Airstream Bambi. Notice the rather sizable Christmas tree visible through the coach window. $5-10.

Art Postcard. Standard glossy card stock, reproduction of watercolor illustration, 5.5" x 4.25", by Bristish artist Annabel Tarrant, unnumbered, 2010. Entitled: *Lovestream*. For Valentine's Day, the Airstream Bambi on this whimsical card had heart-shaped windows. $5-10.

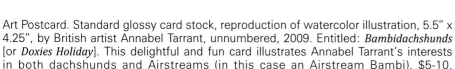

Art Postcard. Standard glossy card stock, reproduction of watercolor illustration, 5.5" x 4.25", by British artist Annabel Tarrant, unnumbered, 2009. Entitled: *Bambidachshunds* [or *Doxies Holiday*]. This delightful and fun card illustrates Annabel Tarrant's interests in both dachshunds and Airstreams (in this case an Airstream Bambi). $5-10.

Holiday Art Postcard. Standard glossy card stock, reproduction of watercolor illustration, long 8.25" x 3.75", by British artist Annabel Tarrant, unnumbered, 2009. Entitled: *Happystream*. Printed greeting on the reverse side: "May the joy of the season live in your hearts all year long." This card is one of our personal favorites because of its details. It showed two holiday gift stockings tied to the Airstream awning support, two dachshunds admiring the impressive and lengthy tandem-axle Airstream Sovereign, the traditional Airstream-blue color on the awnings and detailing of the coach, and a tiny Christmas tree on the counter inside the Airstream. $5-10.

Art Postcard. Standard glossy card stock, reproduction of watercolor illustration, large 8.8" x 5.5", by British artist Annabel Tarrant, unnumbered, 2010. Entitled: *Summerstream*. This playful card has daisies growing on the ground around the Airstream Bambi and daisies on the curtains and awning of the Bambi itself. $5-10.

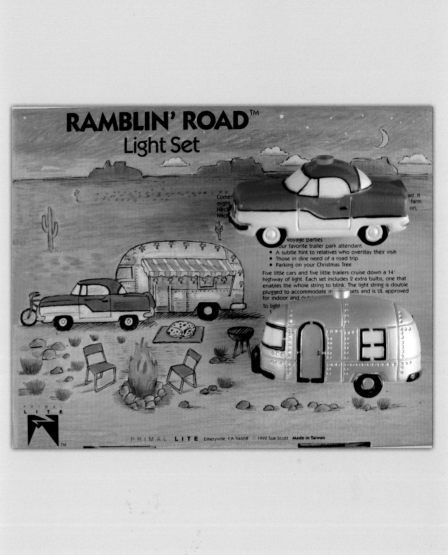

Art Postcard. Standard glossy card stock, reproduction of watercolor illustration, large 8.5" x 5.5", by British artist Annabel Tarrant, unnumbered, 2011. Entitled: *Relaxevoustream*. This cute card depicts both the detailed exterior of an Airstream Bambi and some of the details of the inside of the coach, such as the black-and-white checkerboard flooring, bright red kitchen cabinet and counter top, and the two-bench dinette. A lady sits peacefully in a lawn chair outside the coach [hence, the title for the piece]. $5-10.

RV Light Set Cover. Cardboard box packaging & plastic light set, multi-color graphic, 11" x 8.5", by Sue Scott & Primal Lite, unnumbered, copyright 1992. Caption: "Ramblin' Road Light Set." Fun and too cute! We have already seen the front cover of this box in the earlier chapter about "Airstream Aerials." Here, the creative and colorful graphics on the back cover of the box illustrate a small car and Airstream trailer parked comfortably in the desert, with a bicycle for riding, a campfire and chairs, a grill for cooking, and a dog asleep on a small rug. We have positioned one pair of the colorful plastic cars and trailers on the top of the box. For the set, $30-40.

Magazine Cover [underneath]. Standard magazine cover, reproduction of multi-color illustration, 8" x 11", by professional illustrator Brad Cornelius, in *AIRSTREAM LIFE*, Spring 2010. This description of the cover art appeared on page 5 of the magazine: "Our cover depicts a fantasy Airstream flying over the Ohio countryside, drawn by *Airstream Life* illustrator Brad Cornelius. Paying homage to 1960s concert posters, but with a bigger color palette, the fantasy design was what Brad describes as 'a real "Hendrix at the Fillmore" feeling'." See the next two postcards. For the full issue, $5-10.

Collector Card [on top]. Glossy cardboard, real color photo, small 3.5" x 2.5", by Winnebago Industries, #10 of 100 in the series, copyright 1994. Caption: "Winnebago Heli-Home" [helicopter camper introduced in 1976]. Maybe the thought of an Airstream in flight is not so farfetched? The text on the back of this card explained: "This unique 'off road' recreational vehicle enabled the outdoor travel enthusiast to enjoy the speed of air travel with the luxury of more traditional motor homes." In 1994, Winnebago produced a box of 100 collector cards showing historic items of significance to the company. For the box of 100 cards, $20-25.

Advertising Postcard [left]. Unused, real color photo, 5.5" x 3.5", by John Preble, unnumbered, copyright 2000. Caption: "A UFO crashed into this trailer in Abita Springs, Louisiana." Yahoo! Not surprisingly, this clever picture appeared on a fun publicity card for the UCM Museum in Abita Springs. Apparently, an Airstream was targeted by this flying saucer because Airstreams look more streamlined and futuristic than any other travel trailers. The text on the back of the postcard read: "Preserved for all the world to see, this flying saucer and Airstream trailer are displayed in the 'you-see-em museum,' the whimsical roadside attraction located in the Northshore area of New Orleans." Wally Byam and the others in charge at Airstream always possessed good senses of humor, so we suspect those executives presently at the helm must relish this kind of good-natured Airstream publicity. $10-15.

Advertising Postcard [right]. Unused, chrome, 3.5" x 5.5", by John Preble, unnumbered, copyright 2000. Caption: "Wreck of the UFO ... Aliens vs Airstream ... See it at the UCM Museum in Abita Springs, Louisiana." Yahoo, again! This even more colorful card was the humorous companion to the adjacent card. The back of the postcard referred to a crash "into a mobile home," which must be the Airstream trailer. Maybe there was a mid-air collision between the Airstream shown on the magazine cover and the Airstream shown on this postcard? $15-20.

RV Book. Standard cardboard covers & book paper, multi-color graphics & photos, 10" x 8", by Robert Landau & James Phillippi, published by Gibbs M. Smith [cover art by Van Schelt], 79 pages, copyright 1984. Title: *Airstream*. This book is truly an outstanding work of RV history. Like Airstream, the book has withstood the test of time, for it remains one of the most interesting and best references about Airstream—even though it was published in 1984. The artwork on its front cover was striking and memorable, with its bright colors and its symbols of Airstream's international prominence [the pyramids, camel, and zebra]. The cover art was both simple and sophisticated—like the name of the book, just *Airstream*, and like the exterior design of the trailer itself. For the book, $25-50.

Cut-Out Note Cards. Standard greeting card stock, bi-fold cut-out design, real color photo, 8.5" x 3.25" folded [8.5" x 6.5" unfolded], by Jeff Milstein & Paper House Productions, #R110, c. 1970s-80s [trailer from the 1960s]. Fantastic finds! Over the years, we have acquired two of these scarce note or greeting cards. They are among our personal favorites and were made from a cut-out of a photograph. Since each is a fold-out card, each will stand when unfolded. On the back appeared this caption: "Airstream Trailer … 24' Tradewind, circa 1963." The accompanying text on the back commented: "Its style embodies the streamlined characteristics of Art Moderne, a machine-art style characterized by smooth surfaces and rounded corners. Innovative design and aerodynamic engineering assured the Airstream's success." Each, $30-40.

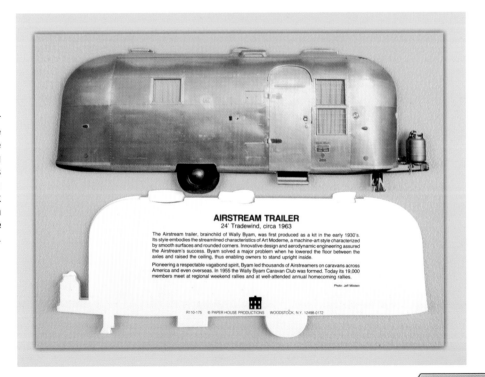

Collector Postcard. Unused, real color photo, 6" x 4.25", by Airstream & Chronicle Books, unnumbered, copyright 2000. Caption: "Adventure Is Where You Find It." This humorous card demonstrated dry, but effective, humor, and showed that the folks at Airstream really appreciated subtle comic relief. The picture revealed an Airstreamer fast asleep while basking in the sun in a hammock on the beach. And, the postcard called it "adventure." Now that's our kind of adventure! $5-10.

Holiday Card. Standard greeting card stock, bi-fold design, multi-color graphics, 7" x 5" folded [7" x 10" unfolded], by Airstream, unnumbered, c. 2000s. Caption: "North Pole." Greeting inside card: "Greetings of the Season and Best Wishes for the New Year." Cute card with a big Airstream and 11 little ones—presumably the big Airstream for the Claus family and the little Airstreams for the elves. $5-10.

Foldout Note Card. Cardboard greeting card stock, fold-out design, multi-color graphics, 5.75" x 4", by Airstream, unnumbered, c. 2000s. This fun note card illustrates a contemporary tandem-axle Airstream trailer. The inside of the card was blank so that a sender could write any type of message in it. After the card was received and read, its recipient could use it as a decoration because it will stand on its own trailer hitch post (as shown). $5-10.

Holiday Card. Standard greeting card stock, bi-fold design, multi-color graphics, 7" x 5" folded [7" x 10" unfolded], by Airstream, unnumbered, c. 2000s. Greeting inside card: "Wishing You every Happiness this Holiday Season and Throughout the Coming Year." Too cute! This whimsical card showed a brightly lighted Christmas tree protruding through a skylight in the roof of the Airstream. $5-10.

Holiday Card. Standard greeting card stock, bi-fold design, multi-color graphics, 5" x 7" folded [10" x 7" unfolded], by Airstream, unnumbered, c. 2000s. Greeting inside card: "Wishing you a Beautiful Holiday Season and a New Year of Peace and Happiness." A fantasy scene with Santa's sleigh in flight, pulling an Airstream along behind. After all, if even a bicyclist could pull an Airstream, then … $5-10.

Foldout Holiday Card. Cardboard greeting card stock, fold-out design, multi-color graphics, 5.5" x 3.5" folded [9" x 3.5" unfolded], by Sandra Lounsbury Foose & The Museum of Modern Art [moma.org], #M250, copyright 2005. Entitled: *Holiday Air Stream*. Greeting printed inside the card: "Reign in the Holiday Spirit!" Fun, festive, & fabulous! This piece was so thoughtfully done in its details. The reindeer that is pulling the trailer, swings into place in front of the coach from inside the card on a pivot point grommet. The borders of the aluminum trailer panels and the rivets are all raised on the card—so that you can run your finger along the card and feel these details. Since we know that a bicyclist can pull an Airstream, a reindeer should certainly be able to tow one as well. How fitting that this card was done in conjunction with The Museum of Modern Art in New York City, since that museum also houses in its collection a 1963 Airstream Bambi. $20-25.

Art Note Card. Standard greeting card stock, bi-fold design, multi-color graphics, 5.5" x 4.25" folded [5.5" x 8.5" unfolded], by artist Richard Neuman [richard-neuman-artist.com], #334, copyright 2001. Amazing! This superbly detailed reproduction of a drawing or painting from The Richard Neuman Print Collection had it all—an American flag, a pair of vintage red lawn chairs, and a fabulous tiny Airstream Bambi, complete with a perfectly realistic wheel and hubcap, propane tank, coffee pot on the counter, two WBCCI emblems on the side of the coach, and more. $20-25.

Comic Postcard. Unused, multi-color chrome, 4" x 6", by Hanna-Barbera Productions & Luna Bay Productions, #J12, copyright 1987. Caption: "Jet-Stream Camper ... Camping Jetsons Style." Space-age fun! No book can possibly be complete unless it includes something from the Jetsons. Here, the scarce card made a wonderful comparison to Airstream—including the grayish sort-of-aluminum color, the rounded not-so-aerodynamic design, the travel stickers on the back section of the coach reminiscent of similar labeling of Airstreams that had traveled in early caravans, and, of course, the "Jet-Stream" name. Humorously, the Jetsons had travel stickers from some fun places like New York, Seattle, Las Vegas, Mount Rushmore, the Grand Canyon—and Pluto, Mars, Venus, and Saturn. $20-25.

Magazine Article [underneath]. Standard magazine paper, full-page, real color photo, 7.75" x 10.5", in *HIGHWAYS*, "Camp Cuisine: Eggs On The Go," by Bob Blumer, March 2005, page 30. This article about a wonderful conversion of a 17' Airstream Bambi into Blumer's "Toastermobile" described the creative transformation of the coach to look like a traveling toaster, complete with two 8' long slices of aluminum toast sticking out of the roof of the unit. Blumer (who was an accomplished cookbook author and host of Food Network's *The Surreal Gourmet*) had a high-tech and high-cost stainless steel kitchen installed in the Bambi [which filled the coach] in order to conduct a promotional tour to publicize his new cookbook. $5-10.

Holiday Card [on top]. Standard greeting card stock, real color photo, folding holiday greeting card, 7" x 5" folded [7" x 10" unfolded], by photographer Liz Kahlenberg Bordow & Palm Press [palmpressinc.com], #X9267, copyright 2001. Printed greeting inside card: "Wishing you the best of all possible holidays!" What a perfectly framed warm-weather scene of a vintage Airstream at the beach for the holidays. $15-20.

124

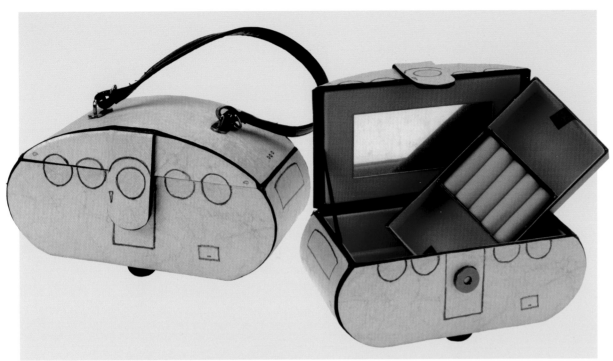

Left: Handled Purse. Folk art lady's handbag with strap handle, 7.5" x 3.5" x 4", no maker, unnumbered, c. 1970s-80s. Wow! Unique one-of-a-kind piece, and incredibly smartly done for a do-it-yourself Airstream look-a-like. If the unknown maker of this purse had made and marketed more of these pieces, s/he could have sold many of them. It is done in the silver-gray color of an Airstream, with a side entry door, a dozen windows, a tow bar, and warning lights drawn onto the coach. $40-50.

Right: Handled Purse. This is the same folk art handbag shown in the accompanying photo, but this view shows the purse in its open position—complete with a small compact mirror and a removable tray for storage above and below.

Carved Sign. Thick soft wood, folk art, large 16" x 11.5", no maker, unnumbered, c. 1960s. Inscription: "Home Is Where You Take It." That caption is in perfect keeping with Wally Byam's philosophy. Curiously, on the back of this hand-carved wooden piece, the following name and dates have been hand-lettered: "H. Moore … 1882 – 1966." We presume this notation is a dedication to someone. Sadly, the artist who so masterfully carved this handsome folk art beauty illustrating a realistic Airstream trailer was not identified. If s/he had been inclined to produce more of them, they would have sold like blueberry hotcakes at a charity pancake breakfast. We feel so fortunate to own what we believe to be the only one of these signs. $75-100.

Top: Art Print. Print of original painting, multi-color, 13" x 8.5", by artist Bob Meredith, #5 of 200, c. 2008. Entitled: *Bob's RV Salvage*. Fantastic nostalgic scene! How many vintage RVs can you count in this picture? Consider the difficulty involved in painting the details of just one or two RVs in most RV paintings. Here, Bob Meredith has illustrated more than 35 vintage RVs in superb detail, most of them modeled after actual coaches owned by members of the Tin Can Tourists organization. He included an Airstream, with its awning extended, in the upper middle area of his piece, but the Airstream looks awfully good to have been relegated to a salvage yard. We bought this print a few years ago from Bob while at a Tin Can Tourists rally in Michigan, and we are so pleased to have it hanging in the foyer of our home in Maine where it greets all of our guests. Bob Meredith's RV art can be seen and purchased on the Tin Can Tourists website at tincantourists.com. For the print, $30-40.

Bottom: Art Print. Print of original painting, multi-color, 13" x 8.5", by artist Bob Meredith, unnumbered, 2009. Entitled: *Cruising By Airstream*. What a clever variation on an Airstream—to fashion it into a pontoon boat. If you look closely, you will see that another Airstream is parked on the shore on the left hand side of the picture. And, like the accompanying work by Meredith, he is not satisfied to have only one RV in the scene. He has included four travel trailers. For the print, $30-40.

Art Print. Print of original watercolor painting, multi-color, 10" x 8", by artist Mary Sundstrom, unnumbered, 2007. Entitled: *Pow Wow*. Striking imagery! The vintage Airstream, with its Native American style curtains, appeared to fit right in amongst the teepees. Perhaps, this outstanding picture suggested symbolism related to the legendary Airstream caravans and rallies, or to the earlier Airstream advertising that sometimes included Native Americans? $30-40.

Art Print. Print of original watercolor painting, multi-color, 10" x 8", by artist Mary Sundstrom, unnumbered, 2010. Entitled: *Just Hanging Out*. Too cute! The relaxed atmosphere of this composition was deceiving. The artist's seemingly simple piece challenged the viewer to notice all of the elements in and about the Airstream that were hidden in plain view—such as the open side window, the tall platform shoes, the two sets of patio/accent lights, the snake-like electric cord, the polka dot apron, the black cat, and much more. $30-40.

BIBLIOGRAPHY

Bailey, Ronald. "Caravans On The Open Road: Home, Home On The Road For A Nation Of Nomads," *LIFE*, Aug. 14, 1970, 20-29 [featuring Airstream caravans].

Banham, Russ. *Wanderlust: Airstream at 75*. Old Saybrook, Connecticut: Greenwich Publishing Group, 2005.

Brunkowski, John & Michael Closen. "Collecting Airstream Postcards," *AIRSTREAM LIFE*, Winter 2009, 12-15.

____. "Collecting Classic RV Toys," *AIRSTREAM LIFE*, Summer 2006, 40-42.

____. "Collecting RV & Camper QSL Cards," *POSTCARD WORLD*, May/June 2012, 20-23.

____. "Motor Coach Postcard Collecting," *FAMILY MOTOR COACHING*, Feb. 2012, 60-63.

____. *Pictorial Guide to RVing*. Atglen, Pennsylvania: Schiffer Publishing, 2010.

____. "RV & Camper Postcards," *POSTCARD WORLD*, May/June 2011, 8-10.

____. *RV & Camper Toys: The History of RVing in Miniature*. Hudson, Wisconsin: Iconografix, Inc., 2008.

____. "RV Toys: Not Just Child's Play," *FAMILY MOTOR COACHING*, Sept. 2006, 92-96.

Burkhart, Brian & David Hunt. *Airstream: The History of the Land Yacht*. San Francisco, California: Chronicle Books LLC, 2000.

Byam, Wally. *Trailer Travel Here and Abroad*. New York, New York: David McKay Company, 1960.

Coldwell, Fred. "The Man Who Defined Airstream Photography: Ardean R. Miller, III," *AIRSTREAM LIFE*, Winter 2007, 36-44.

Evans, Ian. "Airstreams Sprout In South Africa," *AIRSTREAM LIFE*, Summer 2011, 38-40.

Gellner, Arrol & Douglas Keister. *Ready to Roll: A Celebration of the Classic American Travel Trailer*. New York, New York: Viking Studio, 2003.

Gilbert, Bil. "A Home On The Range," *SPORTS ILLUSTRATED*, July 6, 1970, 46-55 [about Airstream caravanning].

Keister, Douglas. *Mobile Mansions*. Salt Lake City, Utah: Gibbs Smith, Publisher, 2006.

____. *Silver Palaces*. Salt Lake City, Utah: Gibbs Smith, Publisher, 2004.

____. *Teardrops and Tiny Trailers*. Salt Lake City, Utah: Gibbs Smith, Publisher, 2008.

Landau, Robert & James Phillippi. *Airstream*. Salt Lake City, Utah: Gibbs M. Smith, Inc., 1984.

Littlefield, Bruce & Simon Brown. *Airstream Living*. New York, New York: Collins Design, 2005.

Lyons, Ted. "You Can Take It With You," *COAST TO COAST*, Sept.-Oct. 1992, 28-31 ["tracing the roots of RVing"].

McClure, Forrest. "The Art Of Airstream," *AIRSTREAM LIFE*, Summer 2009, 38-41.

Miller, Norma. "Through Europe by Trailer Caravan," *THE NATIONAL GEOGRAPHIC MAGAZINE*, June, 1957, 769-816 [with 43 photographs by Ardean Miller].

Smith, Michael. "Airstream Artist Mary Sundstrom," *AIRSTREAM LIFE*, Winter 2007, 23-24.

Spiher, Charles. "Shoebox History: Why Postcard Collecting May Be The Best Way To Remember Your Airstream Travels," *AIRSTREAM LIFE*, Winter 2007, 26-29.

Trailer Coach Homes. Greenwich, Connecticut: Fawcett Publications, 1952.

Winick, David. *Airstreams: Custom Interiors*. Atglen, Pennsylvania: Schiffer Publishing, 2011.

Wood, Donald. *RVs & Campers 1900-2000: An Illustrated History*. Hudson, Wisconsin: Iconografix, Inc., 2002.

Wynne, Nick. *Tin Can Tourists in Florida 1900-1970*. Charleston, South Carolina: Arcadia Publishing, 1999.